"Part narrative, part textbook, and all ei
is a must-read for all anglers wanting t(
fishing. Keep it in your boat, not on y(
            —Mike Zlotnicki, Managing Editor,
            Carolina Adventure Magazine

"I have found *Inshore Angler* by Mike Marsh that is focused along
the Carolina Coast to be both interesting and informative. Every outdoorsman will love these stories."
            —W. Horace Carter, Pulitzer Prize-Winning
                                  Journalist

"Beginners and seasoned fishermen alike will find Mike Marsh's
Inshore Angler a 'must have' guide to Carolina's inshore saltwater
fishing. Not only is this book full of practical tips on how, when,
and where to catch all of the most sought-after coastal fish species,
it's so well written that any fisherman with a pulse will thoroughly
enjoy reading it just for fun."
            —David F. Johnson, Editor,
                North Carolina Game & Fish Magazine

"This isn't just a book, it's a portable fishing seminar. Quoting from
both his own experiences and those of a number of other knowl-
edgeable anglers, the author uses anecdotes to communicate his
thoughts. Simply put, *Inshore Angler* raises the bar for fishing
guidebooks. Marsh serves up top-notch writing, replete with photographs and maps, to offer a guidebook that combines style and
substance."
            —Ken Foster, *Wilmington Star-News*

"Mike Marsh has been one of the premier outdoor writers in North
Carolina for many years. His latest effort is a distillation of some of
his finest works. Anyone hoping to catch fish along the coast would
do well to learn from the lessons in this book."
            —Craig Holt, Managing Editor,
                North Carolina Sportsman Magazine

Inshore Angler

Coastal Carolina's Small Boat Fishing Guide

By
Mike Marsh

Third Edition

Distributed to the book trade by
John F. Blair, Publisher
Winston-Salem, NC 27103

Inshore Angler by Michael S. Marsh

Distributed to the book trade by
John F. Blair, Publisher
1406 Plaza Drive
Winston-Salem, NC 27103
(336)768-1374 or Toll free (800)222-9796 Fax(336)768-9194
www.blairpub.com

First color edition 2000
First black & white edition 2004
Second black & white edition 2007

09 08 07 06 05 04   6 5 4 3 2 1

Library of Congress Cataloging-in-Publication Data:

Marsh, Mike, 1953—
        Inshore angler: coastal Carolina's small boat
fishing guide/by Mike Marsh.—
        1st ed.
        p. cm.
        Includes glossary
        ISBN: 1-928556-21-3 (2000 color edition)
        ISBN: 1-928556-43-4 (2004 b&w edition)
        ISBN: 978-1-928556-43-4 (2006 b&w edition)
        1. Fishing—North Carolina—Guidebooks. 2. North
        Carolina—Guidebooks. I. Title.
        SH531.M38 2000   799.1'66148—dc21   00060342

Photographs by Mike Marsh
Maps courtesy of Maptech
Book and cover design by Jane Baldridge Fisher/Artspeaks

Printed in Canada

In memory of
Curtis Leroy Marsh Jr. and Curtis Arthur Marsh,
my first fishing buddies.

Acknowledgements

Although the author is the only person lucky enough to sign his name to a book, any project of such great magnitude is the result of a team effort by many. *Inshore Angler* is no exception and I would like to thank the following people for their generous contributions:

Guides who shared their knowledge and showed the way to many successful trips out on the water - Tyler Stone, Jimmy Price, David Mammay, Lee Parsons, Bill Douglas, and Doug Cutting.

Tackle shop owners who freely gave their tips on tackle and the locations of many fishing hot spots - Terry Burch, Tex Grissom, Steve Lebanac, and Rob Pasfield.

Anglers who shared my luck on good days and bad or shared their stories - Phil Pare, Ned Connelly, Butch Spivey, Wayne Cook, Steve Laughinghouse, Vinnie Tomaselli, Charles Dycus, and Chris Robbins.

Biologists who gave insight into the management and life cycles of fish - Chris Moore and Louis Daniel.

People who posed for photos or snapped the shutter release when I had my hands full of fish or tackle - Joey Hill, David Boylston, Deedee Harris, Brandon Keith, Leslie Britt, Vicky Rae Frederick, and Buddy Connelly.

The folks at Coastal Carolina Press, with special thanks to my editor, Ellen Rickert, for tidying up.

Jane Baldridge, who worked miracles while designing this book.

The wonderful folks at Maptech, who generously provided base maps for showing the locations of fishing hot spots and boat ramps.

To Justin Marsh and Carol Marsh go my love, admiration, and special thanks. When someone writes a book, they live with it until it seems to become part of their family. Anyone who reads *Inshore Angler* will see that my family has done an enormous amount of work to bring its wisdom to our fellow fishermen who ply the brine in tiny craft.

Inshore Angler
Coastal Carolina's Small Boat Fishing Guide

Table of Contents

July-September

October-December

Introduction

Inshore Angler is written for fishermen who travel North Carolina's section of the Atlantic Intracoastal Waterway and the state's rivers, sounds, inlets and marshes in small boats. Its purpose is to give small boat anglers the knowledge they need to become successful at catching the most popular game fish available along the state's coast, including black drum, bluefish, bonito, cobia, false albacore, flounder, red drum, Spanish mackerel, spotted sea trout, striped bass, and weakfish.

A variety of fishing techniques is discussed, with tips from some of the state's top inshore fishing guides as well as from Marsh himself. Some of the chapters also include information about the biology and management of the fish. The chapters are compiled in edited form from some of the most popular magazine articles written by the author.

Not only do the chapters tell small boat anglers when and where to catch fish, they also include photographs, maps and detailed descriptions of the gear, bait and lures that guides use as well as the locations of many of these professional anglers' favorite fishing spots. Once an angler reads the description of these special honey holes, he can apply his new knowledge to his home waters and become as successful as the pros.

The chapters about catching individual species of fish are organized into three-month cycles roughly showing the time each fish is most available or when the particular technique discussed for catching the fish is most productive. However, weather patterns, current patterns, and the wide range in latitude between the various areas along the state's coastline where these fish species occur can disrupt any attempt to predict when and where they will arrive and depart in any particular area. The three-month cycles shown should therefore serve the inshore angler as general guidelines. For up-to-the-minute information, anglers should contact their local sources of information including tackle shops, guides and fellow recreational anglers.

Marsh said, "I became a writer to learn as much as I can about hunting and fishing. My goal is to make my readers more successful so they will come away from each trip to the outdoors with a renewed appreciation for the natural world and help to protect it for our children's future enjoyment."

Inshore Angler makes a long cast in that direction.

Mike Marsh with a big red drum caught on a jig as proof that anglers fishing multiple rods from small boats catch some of the finest saltwater game fish.

Anglers in johnboats and skiffs line up along Wrightsville Beach jetties to cast for speckled trout and red drum.

Chapter 1

Universal Boats—Evolution and Selection of Johnboats and Skiffs

An inshore angler's mind often wanders, daydreaming of a perfect, universal boat that is seaworthy enough to trust on an excursion for puppy drum in wind-chopped waves alongside a barnacle-encrusted jetty, or skim across an oyster bar in inches-deep water for a surf fishing adventure on a barrier island.

If the fisherman's dream craft is to be trailered to its launching point, the lightweight of an aluminum johnboat makes the towing and launching easy, even with a very small vehicle. Fly-fishermen, duck hunters and flounder giggers can find no better design than a 16-foot flat-bottomed johnboat for poling through a marsh on low water. Those who travel coastal rivers and the Atlantic Intracoastal Waterway searching for speckled trout will find a semi-V, aluminum hull in 16- to 19-foot length more suitable for negotiating choppy boat wakes and inlet breakers. These larger designs are also navigated regularly as far as three miles offshore on calm days. The hulls are so light they ride on top of swells like a cork instead of crashing through them like heavier craft.

Some anglers argue about the difference between johnboats and skiffs. The dictionary definition of a "skiff" is a rowboat or small, open sailing vessel that is light enough to be rowed with ease. However, that archaic definition has been expanded upon by many boat manufacturers and anglers who use small outboards to power today's shallow-draft craft, collectively called skiffs, that are capable of performing any task - from setting and retrieving nets, to dredging clams and oysters, collecting crab pots, or hook-and-lining game fish.

The first Carolina plank-built skiffs were made from Atlantic white cedar or juniper. The shipwright's craft of the time and the limitations of the materials resulted in lightweight, seaworthy vessels that sported high bows to cut waves and a fore-to-aft "rocker" to ride a heavy chop by rolling rather than pounding against the waves.

Eventually, the Carolina-style bow became synonymous with quality boats the world over. Modern materials made the boats lighter and more durable. Fiberglass laid over lap-strake siding with the strakes overhanging one another to dissipate the energy of a wave rising upward against the hull created a much-needed improvement that brought boats within the price-range of recreational boaters who did not need to earn a living on the water.

Finally, small boats evolved into the present day's marvelous miracles of lightweight resins. Anti-fouling paints add to their durability by defeating encrusting organisms. My personal, modern definition of a skiff is any lightweight aluminum, wood or fiberglass boat of shallow draft design that can be rowed, poled or pushed by one or two men in water too shallow for an outboard to run. Sportsmen of the Carolinas are blessed with a wide selection of such boats in a variety of hull configurations.

Flared-bow skiffs are the most seaworthy in rough conditions. The Jones Brothers Cape Fisherman is one of the most recent examples of this type of skiff, and is manufactured in several lengths to be suitable for nearly any size water. Other North Carolina manufacturers also offer this type of hull.

While the flared bow may cut the chop from rough seas, it is not the best choice for anglers needing a forward deck for throwing a cast net or casting a fly line. Since these are major activities performed by serious sportsmen, the definition of a skiff tends to narrow each year toward a flat-bottomed, flat-bowed wood and fiberglass boat. Southern Skimmer in Havelock, McKee in Fairmont, Sea Sport in Cornelius and Jones Brothers in Morehead City are some of the best-known North Carolina manufacturers building this type of skiff. Carolina Skiff of Waycross, Georgia builds one of the most popular boats of this type. This list includes just a few of the many manufacturers that build flat-bottomed skiffs across the nation and sell them through North Carolina dealers. These flat-bottomed boats would have been impossible to build with any durability if wood was still the sole manufacturing material available. However, modern resins cast in molds now support decks of super-strong plywood covered with resin. The decks are then stippled or painted with non-skid paints, enabling them to take quite a pounding while giving their crews a relatively soft, secure and stable ride.

Skiffs come in various rigging and steering configurations, and most can be custom-ordered to a customer's specification. For example, since I am both a waterfowl hunter and fishermen, my 19-foot, 8-inch Jones Brothers Bateau sports an olive green hull for camouflage. It has an offset console to keep it out of the way when shooting from a sitting position on the floor or when collecting decoys. The offset console also allows two anglers to pass one another on the same side of the boat when fighting and netting a fish. A grab rail and windshield are attached to the console.

A storage compartment in the bench seat extends gunwale to gunwale. A forward deck provides a platform for casting a net and has storage underneath for storing anchors, line and gear. Horizontal rod holders keep up to four rods safe along the gunwales, and twelve upright holders keep live-bait and trolling rods instantly available from any angler's position.

The whole rig draws about six inches of water, unloaded, and is self-bailing. My personal choice in skiff model and style is just one example of one Carolina manufacturer's boat, and each builder offers a boat that is unique based on his experiences and talents.

My johnboats have worn aluminum skins for decades. Although I still own an aluminum boat for towing overland to remote destinations, the Jones Brothers Bateau that resides in the water at my dock is a flat-bottomed skiff that has a fiberglass hull. When the Environmental Protection Agency (EPA) mandated removal of tin from bottom paints a few years ago, it forced me to buy a fiberglass hull. Tin-based paints once protected aluminum hulls from encrustations and galvanic action for as long as three years. However, with the fast-scouring type of coatings that are the only reliable present choice for protecting aluminum hulls, six months protection is all that can be relied upon today. Fiberglass boat hulls can be protected with copper-based anti-fouling paints that are readily available and are therefore the best choice for leaving in the water for extended periods of time.

Although several manufacturers offer huge, fiberglass johnboats, 20 feet is about the maximum length for a fiberglass johnboat to be used by a single angler in quiet sounds and bays due to weight considerations. However, a 16-footer can be more easily manhandled off an oyster bed or maneuvered onto a trailer in a side wind. The best fiberglass skiff hull designs are flat or nearly flat with bottom chines or a center keel for grabbing water to prevent them from side slipping in a turn.

Outboard horsepower can run from 15 hp on small aluminum hulls to 90 hp on larger fiberglass boats. The lightest motor that will reliably plane the hull with a full load is the best choice. Power tilt-and-trim for motors above 30 hp is required because tilting heavier motors by hand is difficult. A hydraulic motor lift or "jack plate" as is used on Florida-style flats boats is a good option for cruising tidal creeks because it allows higher speeds with greater maneuverability than relying on a tilt-and-trim. Some anglers who really want to get up in the shallows use jet drive outboards. However, these motors have high rates of maintenance because the drive mechanisms can become clogged with vegetation and sand.

Steering options for small boats range from a simple tiller handle on a twist-grip throttle, to a steering wheel on a sit-down console or a center console. While a center console keeps the captain dry and allows stand-up vision on boats designed for large water bodies, it is an obstruction to fish around, adds lots of weight, and is nearly impossible to hide in short marsh grass while duck hunting. The sit-down console is probably the best compromise for boats that will seldom be used offshore.

Lockable hatch covers on the console to shield a depth recorder and switch panel are handy add-ons as are vertical rod holders to prevent damage to fragile fishing rods. Live wells are mandatory on the fully equipped inshore boat. Moveable plastic live wells are good options in these smaller craft because they can be situated in various locations until just the right position is found to counterbalance the weight of the water in the well. Paired rod holders at fishing stations on each gunwale are a great source of convenience. One rod holder can hold a live bait rig, while its mate is open for frantically stabbing a plugging rod into when snatching up the live bait rod and setting the hook on a strike.

A forward deck increases hull weight and draft. However it is essential equipment. From a forward deck, casting a net is a simple task, retrieving anchors is easy, and some anglers find that a trolling motor attached to a forward deck is an asset when casting lures for fish in calm areas. While seldom seen in the past on Carolina sound boats, Florida-style poling platforms that are located above the outboard motor are becoming a popular item, especially among fly-fishermen.

A live well with an intake and a discharge point outside the boat hull keeps baits frisky. Dual pumps and dual batteries guarantee that baits will stay alive. Single pump systems without backup batteries can malfunction at unfortunate times. Without backup, a fishing trip can be ruined when delicate baitfish like menhaden turn belly-up from lack of oxygen.

Lockable storage seats are nice options. Rods and guns stored inside these compartments stay undamaged and odds and ends that might otherwise remain ashore remain onboard at all times.

Anchors fore and aft are required equipment for holding small boats securely against waves, currents and wind. Excess anchor rope should be coiled around paired cleats on gunwales or in a bow locker. If not properly stored, rope gets tangled around feet and grabs wayward treble hooks so well that they may have to be cut free.

Fixed bow lights are standard equipment, while rear lights can be mounted on top of the motor cowl, or removable design, or of fold-down design.

Self-bailing decks on most of today's fiberglass boats work well. Scuppers valve water out that enters over the gunwales while keeping backwash out. But there always seems to be a little slosh under-foot because scupper valves don't close instantly, so a bilge pump set in a sump well and plugs for the scupper drains are convenient extras for a self-bailing boat. For single-hulled aluminum johnboats, a bilge pump located at the transom is a nice convenience. However, when a johnboat is running on plane, simply removing the drain plug allows water to drain from inside the hull.

This float rig baited with a live shrimp caught speckled trout, jacks, bluefish and croakers from the same location in a creek mouth.

Chapter 2

Prospecting for Fish Using the Three-Rod Method

While anchoring the boat along the edge of a jetty, Ned Connelly surveyed the current scouring the oyster-encrusted boulders and creating eddies and swirls between gaps in the seawall. Dip-netting a menhaden from the live well and hooking it through the roof of the mouth, he lowered the wriggling bait on a slip-sinker rig to the bottom, twenty feet beneath the surface. The one-ounce weight bounced until it tightened the line and put a steady bend in the rod.

Netting a live shrimp from the bait tank, I impaled it through the horn on its head with a No. 6 treble hook. A split shot held the shrimp at a depth of four feet beneath a weighted, casting float. Cast up current, the float skirted the jagged rocks. As I set the rod in a holder, the shrimp flipped its tail, making the float dance as it flirted with the disaster of a cut-off line.

While I tied a MirrOlure on the line of a second rod, Ned cast a leadhead jig with a plastic grub tail. Watching the baited lines as we cast along the seawall, we covered every nook and cranny with our lures in case the live-bait offerings were snubbed by the game fish.

After several casts with no strikes, I dropped a Carolina rig to join Ned's rig on the bottom. Ned set out a float rig like mine.

"How do you know there are any fish here?" Ned asked.

"I don't. At this point, we're just prospecting," I replied.

We had tried the same tactics without success at other places in the past hour – along a series of docks, at a sandbar in an inlet and along a grass bed. However, on some days fish are scattered or just plain picky about where they will concentrate or what they will eat.

Suddenly, Ned lifted his rod to set his hook. Jerking hard met zero resistance as he reeled in a tailless grub.

Before he could say "bluefish" my float rod bent double as a chopper blue launched like a Polaris missile with the treble hook in his mouth and the float leaping from the water behind him. Setting my plugging rod in a holder, I asked Ned to reel in the line as I played the bluefish. But a strike on his bottom rod demanded attention before he could do anything else but drop his plugging rod into a holder.

Ned's fish surged along the sandy bottom, while my bluefish surfed on top to the boat. I netted the bluefish, then reeled in the plugging rods that dangled lures over the side. Reeling in my bot-

This bottom rig baited with a live shad will catch striped bass and red drum.

tom rod, I let out line on Ned's remaining float rig, until it was beyond danger of entangling the line connected to the fish. After a hard-fought battle, Ned eventually boated a ten-pound red drum. Before we freed the fish from the net, a speckled trout hit the remaining float rig.

"I think we hit the mother lode," Ned said.

Releasing the drum, Ned made the landing net available for my trout. Before the morning was over besides catching drum, trout and bluefish, we also caught flounder, croakers and assorted bait-stealers like pinfish and pigfish. But it took a lot of searching to narrow down the fishing area to find this pocket of productive water.

So it goes for all anglers who ply the brine. The race is always on to find fish before running out of fishing time. But many anglers spend too much time in unproductive areas and do not test the full depth of the water at most locations for the entire spectrum of the many species that are lurking there. Over the years, I have discovered that the "three-rod method" is the most effective approach to prospect for fish.

The three-rod method requires a weighted line to drop a natural bait to the bottom, a floating line to suspend a natural bait between the bottom and the surface, and a casting line to present lures on the surface and to areas that cannot be reached by the baited lines. The types of rods selected are not important. All styles of reels and all line weights are candidates for this system. Some anglers find a revolving spool reel works for the bottom line, while the best rod for casting lures is a spinning rig. This method works just as well for offshore fishing as it does for skinny water angling. Only two things are required to make the three-rod method work – good rod holder placement and systematic rod handling.

For a pair of anglers to fish three rods each, twelve rod-holders are required on a boat. There should be a trio of double-holders fore, amidships and aft on each side of the boat. It seems that a casting rod could be inserted into a holder left vacant when a live bait rod is removed to set its hook. However, it takes both hands to fight a fish at initial hook-set. Also, if a plugging rod is merely set down in the boat when a fish strikes on another rod, it may be stepped on or launched over the gunwale if a fish strikes a lure or a bait left dangling in the water.

The reason for positioning holders on both sides of the boat is that the wind and current dictate which side of the boat must be fished. When fishing a visible structure such as a jetty, a switch of the tide from rising to falling swings an anchored boat 180 degrees. If the holders are all on the opposite side of the boat from the structure, the angler is out of business in that particular spot.

When arriving at a fishing spot, the bottom rig is set first. The line goes down current, since that is where it will wind up eventually no matter where it is cast. The drag is set light enough for the warning clicker to alert the angler when a fish strikes.

The float rig is set out next. The bait can be cast down current or downwind of the boat or into the current or wind to allow it to drift beside fish-holding cover such as a grass bed or dock. The advantage of a float rig is that the float gives a visible indication of a strike when it is pulled beneath the surface. The float can also be adjusted on successive casts to present the bait at different water depths. The reel drag should be set light enough to easily engage the warning clicker, because the float cannot be watched all the time when casting other lines.

After setting out the two baited rods, an angler should wait a few minutes before casting lures with the third rod. If lots of fish are in the area, live baits will produce immediately. However, if action is slow, the angler can begin casting to areas of visible structure or jigging along the bottom with a plugging rod, allowing quick exploration of areas where the live bait rigs cannot reach.

When a fish hits, it is imperative to clear remaining lines out of the way. This is when it pays to have a partner. The first few seconds can spell the difference between a boated fish and tangled lines.

The worst offenders are bottom lines. Any line connected to a hooked fish circling the boat is certain to snag them. Once the angler who is not fighting the hooked fish reels in his lure, he should reel in the bottom lines. Live baits can be dunked — hook, line and sinker — into the live well or left suspended a couple of inches into the water beside the boat to keep them alive. If the fish being fought can be worked to the boat quickly, the float lines can be left overboard or given more line to clear them out of the fighting zone. Since floats are easy to see, the fish can be worked around them. If they must be cleared, such as when fighting long-running jumpers like bluefish, they should be moved to the opposite of the boat from the side the fish is fought and landed or they should also be removed from the water.

When fishing alone, the angler who has a strike on a lure faces the worst-case scenario for tangling lines. Although no technique for keeping fish clear of the two overboard lines is foolproof, the best method is keeping as much distance as possible between baits at the outset. The bottom rig goes right under the boat, reducing the number of one-hand reel turns required to bring the bait up while holding a rod being used to fight a fish in the opposite hand. The float rig is allowed to drift a long distance from the boat so it won't interfere in a battle. It also helps to spread rods, fore and aft, or on opposite sides of the boat so that more water is clear when a fish is hooked on any of the rods.

There will be times when one of the three rods is so productive that it is the only one that can be fished. Indeed, the discovery of which method is most effective for the species present in a particular area is the goal of the three-rod approach. If an angler were only casting a surface popper, he would not know that flounder are so numerous on the bottom they are laying on top of one another. He also would not know that speckled trout are schooling at the edge of a nearby grass bed while he presents only a chunk of a cut bait on the bottom.

That's the beauty of prospecting for fish by using three rods. Every game species is targeted, at every water depth in one location. With such a smorgasbord available, it only takes a few minutes to eliminate the question of whether a spot is just "fishy looking" or if it actually holds fish.

The author demonstrates the use of a 10-foot cast net to catch live minnows and shrimp.

Lots of practice with a cast net results in perfect throws that catch bait quickly.

Chapter 3

How To Catch Saltwater's Best Live Baits

Sunrise was no more than a promise as our boat slipped into the mouth of a tidal creek. Although it was not raining, the water's surface rippled as if being pummeled by a hailstorm, a sure sign of a big school of baitfish.

With one cast of the net, I captured enough of those menhaden "hailstones" for several hours of fishing. The baitfish were schooling so tightly that the net could not sink. Instead, it rose to the surface under their collective swimming.

My eight-year-old son, Justin, giggled as the flipping fish showered the deck from the open net and slithered through his fingers. He tossed them into the live well and saved the last to bait his hook. The

A good cast with the net resulted in these shrimp to use as bait. Shrimp are the best bait for speckled trout.

minnow hadn't settled to the bottom when a flounder struck it. Before it was even time for breakfast, the main ingredient of a flounder dinner was flapping its tail against the bottom of our ice chest.

Justin was learning the saltwater angler's trade and one of the most important tools for success in the brine is the knowledge of how to catch the right baits. Sometimes the search for bait can consume more time than the actual hours spent angling. The upside to all that searching is that catching bait often is as much fun and challenge as catching a game fish.

When anglers associate saltwater with fish bait, they usually think of minnows. Indeed, there are many species of small fish that make excellent baits. The most desirable of these species are mullet and menhaden because of their habits of schooling in open water, making them easy targets for cast nets. Cast nets are thrown from a bank, dock or boat and are available in many diameters and mesh sizes.

Cast net sizes are referred to by radius. For example, a six-foot net is actually twelve feet in diameter. Nets of three to six feet have small bar sizes of 1/4 to 3/8-inch and are used to capture small baits used for inshore species, such as flounder, drum, speckled trout, bluefish and Spanish mackerel. Larger nets of up to fourteen feet, with bar sizes up to 3/4-inch, are used to capture adult menhaden and mullet for targeting offshore species like king mackerel. The larger mesh allows the net to sink faster in deep water to capture great numbers of large schooling baitfish.

While mullet and menhaden are the mainstays for catching most game fish, other finfish, such as mud minnows, killifish, pinfish, pigfish, spots and croakers, will also work well as bait when menhaden or mullet are scarce. Menhaden and mullet are free swimming. These other baits, however, are structure-oriented. Killifish and mud minnows are caught in creek channels at low tide when they are forced to leave surrounding grass beds. They are also caught near ocean inlets and sandbars on higher tides, when they can be seen swimming against the light-colored sand at the water's edge.

Pinfish, croakers and spots congregate around docks, sea walls and oyster beds. Accuracy with a cast net is important when casting near hard structure or the net will become fouled on oyster shells, resulting in a gaping hole cut in the mesh. The only way to learn how to cast a net accurately is by reading instructions, learning from another angler or watching a video, then practicing until the net not only lands over the target area, but misses obstructions with its edges.

One tip for getting the most out of practice sessions is to cast the net onto a lawn from a picnic table instead of across the water from

Phil Pare unloads popeye mullet from his cast net. These mullets are finger sized—just right for catching flounder or speckled trout.

the bow of a boat. The net is lighter during multiple casts because it stays dry. This prevents fatigue, especially when using nets of over six feet. Nets of ten feet and above can weigh more than twenty pounds when dry. Not many anglers can make more than a dozen casts with these large nets, so it pays to practice before heading out to the water.

One of the best places to catch croakers, pinfish and spots is near a fish-cleaning station on a dock or at a seafood-processing house, where the supply of ready-made chum keeps these little predators schooling. Tossing canned pet food into the water near a recreational dockside fish-cleaning station ensures that a net full of bait will be easy to catch because the fish are always waiting nearby hoping for a handout.

If an angler cannot use a cast net due to snags or unfamiliarity with casting techniques, he can resort to hook and line. A tidbit of shrimp on a No. 6 hook will catch small "bait stealers." Kids really come in handy for catching a bucket full of pinfish, and they enjoy catching the bait as much as catching game fish because it is so easy.

Snagging certain baits with rod and reel also has its place, especially out in the open ocean waters where a school of alewife, cigar minnows or menhaden suddenly appears on the surface. A treble hook is tied to the line with a sinker about six inches below. Cast with a spinning rod, the hook and weight are reeled and jerked quickly through the school until a fish is snagged.

A passive device for catching small baits is a minnow trap, which is a wire mesh cylinder with a funnel entrance at both ends. Bait is placed in the trap and the trap is tied to a bulkhead or staked in an opening in a grass bed. A fish head makes a minnow trap bait that will last several days, although all of the bait necessary for a day's fishing can be caught within a single tide change. Mud minnows and juvenile fish enter creek channels and depressions on low tide. Setting the trap in such a depression where it will remain submerged when the tide is at its lowest point ensures that the bait will be alive when the trap is checked. Many anglers have a favorite place for setting minnow traps and let them remain in place for the entire fishing season.

Live shrimp are great baits for speckled trout, drum, croakers, spots, pompano, bluefish and many other species. The difficult thing about using shrimp is that it takes many dozens to last a day of fishing because everything that swims eats them

Shrimp can be caught with cast nets. They congregate in creek channels and depressions in tidal flats during low tide and in the edges of grass beds on higher tides. Shrimp seen flipping out of the water to avoid predators can be caught by sight casting. However, when shrimp are scattered, they can be concentrated into a small area with bait. Some anglers mix fish-

Carol Marsh sets a minnow trap near a bulkhead. The floating bait bucket on the boat deck will help keep them alive all day.

meal or pet food with garden clay. They put these "shrimp balls" out in likely places in the marsh and mark the locations with white plas-

Blue crabs can be caught in traps and make excellent bait for many species of game fish.

tic plumbing pipe. After waiting an hour, the angler returns, casts the net one time and has a day's supply of shrimp.

My favorite method for catching shrimp is placing canned cat food inside the toe of a lady's sheer stocking and suspending it beneath a dock. Whenever I need shrimp, I simply cast a net beneath the stocking.

Crabs should not be overlooked as baits. Tiny mole crabs that scamper in the surf are great baits for sheepshead, pompano, croakers, red drum and black drum. They can be gathered by hand, but a rake with a wire mesh basket will collect them faster and keep the angler dry.

Other small crabs that make great baits are the half-dollar-sized rock crab and fiddler crab. Rock crabs are gathered by hand and are found by lifting erosion-control stones or driftwood. Fiddler crabs parade by the millions on mud flats at low tide and are also collected by hand.

The larger blue crabs make great baits for tarpon, red drum, black drum and cobia. These are testy critters and are definitely not gathered by bare hands. Blue crabs are caught in crab pots baited with fish and placed in channels or suspended under docks. They are also caught with hand lines baited with fish heads or chicken necks. The bait is tossed into the water and slowly worked back. Blue crabs hold on to the bait until the bait nears the surface. A net slipped under the crab catches it before it lets go.

For handling large crabs, especially potential finger-cutters like blue crabs, it is best to place them immediately on ice to tranquilize them as well as to keep them alive. An iced blue crab is safe to handle. Otherwise, heavy gloves are required. All crabs can be frozen without losing their value as baits.

This striped bass was caught on a fly tied and cast by Captian Tyler Stone.

Chapter 4

Saltwater Fly-Fishing Is Catching On

It was one of those sweltering June afternoons, with the sun beating down on the ocean's mirror-flat surface, reflecting the first orange streaks of sunset against my polarized glasses. Removing them to wipe trickles of sweat from the lenses, I began to re-evaluate the light spinning rig in the rod holder. It had been about as useful as a buggy whip in my attempts at catching the Spanish mackerel that were leaping all around the boat.

A usually productive tinsel jig had not enticed one certain strike, and I probably had just imagined a couple of fish flashing at the lure, reflecting the slanting rays of the sun off their silver flanks. Off the tip of a jetty, I studied an angler hooked up with another mackerel. He had been catching fish continuously, one fish after another, for at least an hour. Cast, catch, release was his routine, with the greatest emphasis on the casting. He was using a *fly rod* of all things, and his success put my feeble efforts to shame.

As he began to stow his gear to head home, I pulled alongside his boat to see why he had caught dozens of fish, while my fish box held only a "skunk."

"Tyler Stone," he introduced himself as he shook my hand. Turns out, he was a fishing guide and also owned a tackle shop that sold only saltwater fly-fishing gear, which was amazing in itself, since just a decade or two ago, the mere thought of such a single-purpose saltwater fishing shop would have been shadowed by night-mares of bankruptcy.

"These Spanish are feeding on tiny glass minnows," he explained, peeling one off the deck where it had been ejected by a hooked fish. "Spanish are very size-selective. There's just no way you could have cast as small a lure as this Deceiver using your tack-le."

I fingered the elegant bit of fluff and studied the long rod from which it dangled.

"This is an expensive rod," he said in response to my look of longing. "But a good, all-around saltwater rig, from the reel right on down to the fly, will only cost in the range of $200 to $250, which is not any more than a good bass rig. The cost of modern gear is one of the main reasons so many fly-fishermen are taking to the salt in record numbers. Presenting ultra light lures with a greater degree of accuracy to surfacing fish is another."

Stone's "luck" with the finicky Spanish mackerel had me convinced. Stopping in at his shop, I was amazed at the array of gear available specifically for use in salt water. Although there is gear available in every price range, here is a listing of what an angler really needs for catching major inshore species, such as red drum, Spanish mackerel, speckled trout, bluefish, striped bass, bonito or any other fish up to approximately twenty pounds in weight.

An 8-weight rod is fine for starters, and should be mated with a reel of anodized aluminum and an 8-weight fly line. The working parts of the reel should be stainless steel and the drag must be absolutely smooth. High-quality reels utilize cork friction pads in the drag system, while lower-end reels use synthetic pads. The lowest prices for durable reels belong to those with click-type drags made of high-impact plastic.

As far as the durability of the rod goes, many lower-priced graphite rods now come complete with a lifetime unconditional manufacturer's warranty. Saltwater fishing is synonymous with rough seas, so a hard case should be used to protect the rod and reel.

Three basic lines are necessary to fish under most conditions — floating, intermediate sinking and full sinking. Whereas a floating line is the mainstay of freshwater angling, it is considered a specialty line for saltwater fishing. It is easier to cast and retrieve and therefore the best line for beginners because returning line to the surface to make a cast is the most difficult aspect of fly-fishing. For calm days, and when casting to surfacing fish, floating line can't be beat.

The most versatile line is an intermediate sinking line. A weight forward intermediate line is easier to cast than a floating line in the ever-present coastal wind. The line will also sink below wave action to minimize its effects on the lure presentation. Intermediate sinking lines work best when fished at depths of three to six feet.

A full sinking line is considered to be a specialty line in the brine. Lines of this type are used when fishing drop-offs, jetties and offshore wrecks up to thirty feet below the surface. The limiting depth factor is current, which creates much more drag on fly line than on conventional monofilament line due to the fly line's larger diameter.

Some anglers store extra fly lines on interchangeable reel spools. However, extra spools cost around $75. The simplest way to store extra line is to coil it around the fingers, then secure the coiled line with twist ties. The line can then be stowed in a tackle box.

The fly line is tied to the reel with a braided Dacron backing line of 20-pound-test. On an 8-weight reel, this provides approximately 200 total yards of line, which is adequate for medium inshore and light offshore use. Besides providing extra line while playing a fish, the backing also increases arbor diameter, giving a higher retrieve ratio. With no gear reduction mechanism, as is the case with conventional reels, direct-drive fly reels require fast finger work, so the reel should be filled with backing to its maximum capacity.

Using a tapered leader allows the fly to "turn over." In the fashion of the sting at the end of a bullwhip, a tapered leader lets the fly land at the end of the line, not in a spider web tangle. Tapered monofilament fly leaders manufactured for saltwater use are harder and stiffer than freshwater fly leaders. However, tapered leaders are made by extrusion, a manufacturing process that makes them softer than straight leaders. Therefore, when fishing for such toothy monsters as bluefish, most anglers tie their own leaders. A typical leader for an 8-weight setup consists of four parts: three feet of 25-pound monofilament, two feet of 20-pound monofilament, one foot of 16-pound monofilament and three feet of 12-pound monofilament. The 25-pound monofilament is tied to the fly line with a nail knot. The sections are tied together with blood knots and a surgeon's loop is tied at the end of the 12-pound section. An 18-inch leader of 30-pound monofilament connects the fly to the leader using another surgeon's loop in a loop-to-loop connection. One foot of wire can also be used to tie the fly to the leader using an Albright knot. Both types of leaders can also be connected to the 12-pound section by tying them on with a swivel.

Basic saltwater flies are the Clouser minnow and the Deceiver. The Clouser is tied with lead eyes. The weight makes the hook ride point up. This style is best for fishing around structure and prospecting for bottom-huggers like flounder and red drum. The upward sweep of the hook keeps hang-ups to a minimum.

The Deceiver is a weight-neutral fly, with the hook tied to ride point down. This fly is used for schooling fish. Poppers can also be effective when sight-fishing. Jigs are very effective for fishing offshore structure. The important difference between a freshwater fly and a saltwater fly is durability. Saltwater flies are often tied with synthetic materials that lengthen their life span in the razor-sharp jaws of saltwater fish.

When casting from a boat, the biggest problem is preventing snags in a fly line. Keeping the deck free of rails, cleats and other hardware helps. Many anglers find that stripping line into a five-gallon bucket prevents tangles. Wading fishermen use stripping baskets to keep tangles tamed. One accessory that must be included is a synthetic stripping glove to protect the fingers from line friction burns when a fast-running fish like a bonito strikes the fly.

Some anglers start out using fly-fishing gear without ever trying other styles. After watching an expert like Stone cast for Spanish mackerel—a picture of gracefulness against a summer sunset—it is no wonder the sheer beauty of this fishing style lures them into giving it a try. The fish are the same and the techniques for catching them are the same as when using more conventional gear. However, there is more direct contact with the fish, when the line streaks through the angler's hands at the instant of the strike and the long, limber rod bends until it feels like it will break. The direct-retrieve reel forces the angler to wind in slack line like a windmill, with only the drag of the thick fly line and a whispered prayer to keep the hook secure in the jaws of the fish. It all adds up to a greater sense of challenge and to getting into a more personal relationship with each fish. It is exciting! It is exhilarating! It is no surprise that saltwater fly-fishing is catching on.

The author with a striped bass caught from the Cape Fear River.

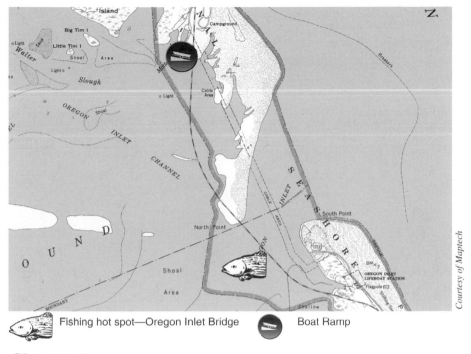

Fishing hot spot—Oregon Inlet Bridge   Boat Ramp

Chapter 5

Sizzling in the Salt - Striped Bass

The return of striped bass to the North Carolina Coast has been nothing short of phenomenal. A decade ago, over-harvest by commercial fishermen and recreational fishermen had reduced striper populations to the point where the catch of a 40-pound linesider was a rare occurrence. However, management plans set in place by fisheries biologists in state waters and federal waters, which included bag limits, quotas on landings and bans on the sale of striped bass have brought them back. Where once the stocked, inland reservoirs of the Carolinas were the best places for catching trophy striped bass, today's anglers are returning to the coastal areas where wild-reared fish are ready to do battle.

Of all the fantastic striper fishing along the coast, the return of the fish to the Albemarle Sound-Pamlico Sound area has been the most outstanding. Once blocking the striped bass spawning run from the sounds, the Roanoke Rapids Lake Dam has provided adequate flow for striped bass to spawn since 1984 thanks to the efforts of the Roanoke Valley Striped Bass Coalition. Restrictions on catches by recreational anglers and commercial fishermen throughout the entire sounds' river systems have really brought back the fish all the way through the sounds and into the Atlantic Ocean. Another factor in restoring the North Carolina striped bass population is the protection of the migratory population that is shared by this region with Chesapeake Bay.

By far, the best place to catch striped bass in spring is Oregon Inlet. In waters just outside the inlet, seeing schools of up to 40-pound striped bass has become a common occurrence. The fish are usually located no deeper than twelve feet below the surface and inside the inlet's sandbar within a few hundred yards of the beach. Fishermen with larger center-console boats can find schooling fish anywhere along the beaches from Kitty Hawk to Cape Point. Small boats are not recommended in this area because the water can stay rough due to constant breezes. Boating access to Oregon Inlet is obtained from the public ramp at the north end of the Herbert C. Bonner Bridge, which spans the inlet from Bodie Island to Pea Island.

Terry Burch, manager of *Fishing Unlimited* tackle shop, said, "Anglers have reported a school of 500-pound giant bluefin tuna feeding on schools of 40-pound stripers just off the beach in January. The twenty-year moratorium on commercial fishing really brought back the fish."

Anglers cast large Hopkins Spoons and natural hair bucktail jigs to surfacing schools near the inlet. When the fish are deeper, trolling lures are used. These lures can be of the swimming minnow type or offshore trolling skirts such as the Sea Witch or Islander skirts with ballyhoos or strip baits attached. These are also the same lures used to catch bluefin tuna in winter.

Mann's Harbor and Alligator River Bridges also offer a striped bass bonanza. These bridges, located near Manteo, have seen a resurgence of stripers for the past several years.

The key to catching these fish is to fish around the bridge pilings during moving water conditions, when the tide is either rising or falling. The area is notorious for rapidly changing weather conditions. An increase in the wind velocity can kick up heavy waves in a short time. Therefore, boats for fishing around the bridges should be at least eighteen feet in length for the safety of the anglers.

The striped bass caught at the bridges typically weigh between two and fifteen pounds. Bait-casting tackle or spinning tackle of medium weight and action for saltwater duty is preferred for catching these fish.

The water depth varies from around five feet near the shoreline to eighteen feet near the centers of the bridges. Therefore, sinking lures such as jigs and spoons are most effective for probing the edges of the bridge pilings.

Fish orient themselves upstream of the wood or concrete pilings, facing upstream into the tidal current in the same manner that freshwater trout suspend in a stream current. Anchoring upcurrent of the bridge and casting directly at the pilings is the best way to begin prospecting for fish. Casting underneath the bridges invites a cut-off

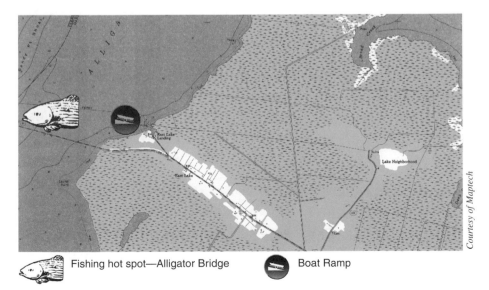

Courtesy of Maptech

Fishing hot spot—Alligator Bridge   Boat Ramp

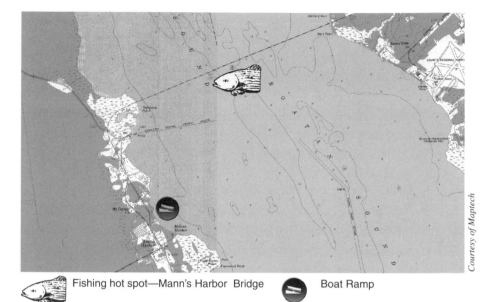

Fishing hot spot—Mann's Harbor Bridge   Boat Ramp

when a powerful fish wraps the line around the pilings. Going with a super braid line instead of using a monofilament line or simply using a length of super braid line for a leader can prevent losing fish from the line chaffing against the barnacles and oyster shells that encrust the bridge pilings.

Access for fishing these bridges is obtained from the ramp at the west end of the Mann's Harbor Bridge at Mann's Harbor Marina and from the east end of the Alligator River Bridge at East Lake Landing.

The Cape Fear River has not seen the restoration of its fishery to the same degree as the fishery in the northern coastal region. Dams on the Cape Fear River restrict spawning migrations and water quality has suffered due to municipal and agricultural runoff. These factors are thought by biologists to limit the spawning success of striped bass. A proposal by the U.S. Army Corps of Engineers to abandon and remove the locks and dams on the river is currently under study. Anglers are hoping that the re-opening of the river will restore the historic spawning runs of stripers and shad.

However, there is still a good number of wild striped bass in the river. Also, recent stockings of "Bodie bass," which are white bass-striped bass hybrids, seems to be working well and fishermen have reported catching large numbers of these fish.

Sea-run stripers weighing above forty pounds are caught with frequency from the Cape Fear River each season. There are always smaller fish in the river system on a year-around basis. However, the giants are usually caught in the period extending from December through March.

Butch Spivey of Wilmington has had a lot of success with the bigger fish in recent years. He fishes hard structure like bridge pilings and old pier pilings above and below Wilmington.

"I use big lures for big fish," said Spivey. "I like a one-ounce red jig head with a large white Mogambo grub. It can be cast around structure, is big enough to attract big fish and can be fished at any depth. It takes a heavy lure to get down to the stripers in the strong current of the Cape Fear River."

Other popular lures are plugs that run from five to fifteen feet deep. Rebel and Rapala stick-minnows, and almost any bass crank bait can catch a striper when trolled around the Exxon dock south of Wilmington and Point Peter, which is located at the junction of the Cape Fear River and Northeast Cape Fear River.

 Fishing hot spot—Smith Creek

At the Exxon dock, anglers troll the shallow flats south of the dock on high tide just south of the dock pilings. At Point Peter, lures are trolled around old pilings along the channel drop-offs on both sides of the river. It is easy to hit a piling or go from ten feet of water depth to zero feet in an instant. The best advice when trolling an area dotted with old pilings is to go slow and go with someone who knows the water. The best way to learn the location of pilings is by observing the area on low tide, then trolling the area on high tide.

Creek mouths that enter the river are good places to try during falling tide conditions. Striped bass school on the upstream sides of the creek mouths to snag minnows as they swim by. Live baits

Courtesy of Maptech

Fishing hot spots—Point Peter, Brunswick River and Town Creek. Boat Ramp

can be difficult to find in spring. However, a small mesh cast net should be kept handy in case a school of alewife or herring on which these stripers feed swims by on the surface. Small minnow traps can also be used to capture eels, which are excellent bait for striped bass.

Live baits are usually fished on the bottom at creek mouths.

However, bottom snags sometimes require that live baits be presented on float rigs.

Some anglers forego live baits for cut mullet and fresh shrimp, which can be bought at any local seafood market. The trick with store-bought bait is making certain it is fresh. Fresh baits can also be used to catch white perch, which are present in the river in February and March. Live white perch make great striper baits and are caught near the Cape Fear River mouth in the deep water at the Archer, Daniels, Midland Corporation (ADM) dock.

Jigs and casting plugs are also good producers at creek mouths. Rat-L-Traps and stick minnows are top lure choices. Wrightsville Beach fly-fishing guide, Tyler Stone, said that Clousers and Deceivers will take stripers from the mouths of creeks. Some of his favored areas are Smith's Creek, Walden's Creek, Town Creek, and the mouth of the Brunswick River.

Besides anchoring and casting in the mouth of Smith's Creek, anglers often motor upstream and cast lures around the bridge at N.C. Highway 132. Trolling the outside banks of the creek channel with shallow-running lures is also productive.

In Walden's Creek, anglers also troll shallow-running plugs. Anchoring and casting at the Sunny Point fence, which blocks the channel in Governor's Creek, is also a good bet. Bucktail jigs are good choices for casting around the fence. MirrOlures are also cast in the area with success.

In Town Creek, anglers often cruise the creek looking for surface-feeding fish. Stick-baits and poppers are deadly when the fish are on top. However, this activity usually subsides with sunrise and begins again at sunset.

Anglers then troll the outside of bends in the creek with deep-running lures. In the tidal creeks, grass fouls hooks often, stealing the action of the lure. Instead of placing the rod in a rod holder, the rod should be held so that any change in lure action can be detected. It also pays to have at least two anglers on board. One angler navigates while the other reels in lines to clean hooks of debris.

It takes an assortment of jigs and lures in a rainbow of colors to consistantly catch finicky spotted sea trout.

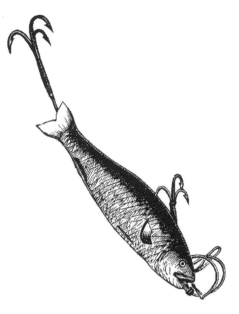

Chapter 6

Sneak Out For Sea Trout

My wife, Carol, made quite a sight as she sat in the bow of the boat with her back to the wind. The hood of her jacket kept the cap from blowing off her head, but the icy pinch of the wind reddened her cheeks while she dabbed at her nose with the back of a neoprene glove. We were far removed from the warmth of civilization and her everyday office attire, so it gave me a grin to see her makeup-bare face highlighted with only Nature's rouge.

"We must be crazy," she said, the words puffing steam clouds for an instant before they disintegrated in the breeze.

Before I could provide proof that we were indeed sane, at least for a couple of speckled trout fishermen, she snatched her fishing rod backward. "Got him!" she shouted as her float dove south. I grabbed the landing net as she played the fish. In a few minutes, I scooped a 3-pound speckled trout from the 45-degree water.

Carol forgot about the blustery weather as her fish went into the ice chest, involving herself instead in hooking another live shrimp on her rig. Casting it overboard to drift above a submerged oyster bed beneath a Styrofoam float produced an instantaneous strike. In the next few hours until the tide changed, we caught enough specks for a feast and let a bunch go free. I couldn't help but point out that the next time we went out in the cold to catch sea trout, she could have an even bigger thrill if she would throw the cast net to catch the bait and give her wet husband a break.

Cabin fever hits anglers especially hard while they wait for the warmth of April to bring back species that migrated with the cold weather. However, spotted sea trout are available to anglers who tough out wintry conditions.

Also called speckled trout or specks, spotted sea trout are colorful and highly prized game fish that are present in estuaries of the Mid-Atlantic states virtually all the year around. However, the summer and fall run of fish are generally "puppies," or yearling fish, and weigh only a pound or two. The trophy "torpedo" trout usually show up in the chill of winter when the water temperature falls into the 50-degree range.

Specks are a fickle fish, seemingly everywhere one season, and extinct the next. Unfortunately, when they do show up, it is always the "you-should-have-been-here-yesterday" story. Trout are actually highly migratory, motivated by temperature and the abundance of prey species. They tend to school in places where their favorite food congregates and follow the bait from place to place.

The seasonal fluctuations of specks are real and not the products of anglers' selective imaginations, which typically remember good years over bad. The latest research shows that specks are very fast-growing fish. Females can achieve a weight of six pounds in a period of only three years. The sounds and bays of the Carolinas and Virginia are the northernmost preferred breeding waters of spotted sea trout. Bitter cold water temperatures along the northern Mid-

Atlantic states, including North Carolina, can destroy the efforts of breeding fish and wipe out whole year-classes, adding credibility to the speckled trout's reputation as a "feast-or-famine" species.

It takes the lure of success to pry an angler's fingers from around the television remote control and replace it with a light, spinning rod, especially when the air temperatures for the day will not top fifty degrees. But the fishermen who know the locations of secret sea trout holes are a tight-lipped bunch who won't easily give out their recipes for success. An angler need not resort to bribery, however, once he learns how to prospect for fish.

Specks congregate around structure and often give away their location by running bait species to the surface if the water is shallow. The edges of grass beds, sandbars and jetties or sea walls are good places for an angler to scout for trout while keeping a sharp eye out for shrimp, menhaden or mullet minnows leaping from the water and piling up against structure in panicked bursts. Trout often chase baitfish to the surface and sometimes expose themselves when they swipe the surface with their backs and tails, although they seldom breach the surface completely.

While looking for evidence of trout feeding, anglers can troll minnow-imitating lures or jigs along the edges of structure. If the fish are deep, trolled lures will find them. Specks are notorious for striking in tiny areas. Therefore, once a strike reveals a feeding fish, an angler can anchor and cast lures or live bait to the location of the strike to entice others in the school.

Wherever another channel, no matter how small, enters a navigable channel, sea trout may be in the area, especially on a falling tide. On rising or high tide, shrimp and minnows feed in grass beds, safely hidden from predators such as sea trout. However, when the tide begins to fall, they use ditches and creeks as highways to gain access to deeper water. Sea trout ambush prey by lying in wait along the deeper water pockets in the channels. Casting lures into the channel at the edge of the grass and working them toward deep holes is a good way to catch those trout. It pays to have several different colors of jigs and plugs when fishing for sea trout. They can be notoriously picky about the colors of lures they will strike on any given day.

In many instances, the switch of the flow at low tide stops the bite, as baitfish find the deepest holes lined with hard structure in which to hide. A hole that is significantly deeper than a surrounding marsh or channel and also has an oyster bed, sunken boat, pilings or other hard structure, is a virtual trout magnet on low tide stages.

Most anglers anchor alongside the shallow edge of the drop-off at the side-current edge of a hole. Casting upstream allows the lure to fall to the level of the structure with the flow of a current. Once the lure passes the structure, working it all the way back to the boat elicits strikes from trout waiting along the edge of the drop-off.

Casting live bait suspended under a float upcurrent and allowing it to drift through a trout holding area is the most efficient way to fish a hole containing hard structure. Not only will the bait be suspended in the strike zone for the entire length of the drift, the length of line beneath the float can be adjusted to prevent the hook from hanging on the structure as it passes above.

While menhaden and mullet minnows attract sea trout, the majority of winter trout are caught using live shrimp for bait. Minnows are hooked through the roof of the mouth with one point of a No. 6 treble hook. A split shot crimped six inches above the bait keeps the bait down in the strike zone, but it should be light enough to prevent the minnow from pulling the float beneath the surface.

Live shrimp are hooked through the horn where it grows from the head. The hook must miss the dark spot, which is the shrimp's brain. If the brain is penetrated, the shrimp will die quickly and will not be as effective as it will if it can swim.

While small live baits, such as minnows and shrimp, attract run-of-the-mill trout and the occasional large fish, there is another heretofore secret bait for catching big "gator" trout. Being curious about feeding habits, I have checked the stomach contents of several fish weighing more than five pounds. Although the fish were caught on live shrimp and lures, each held the remains of pinfish that were four to seven inches in length. A check with a topnotch trout guide,

David Mammay, who operates *Reel Success Guide Service* in Southport, confirmed my suspicion. He said that big trout prefer pinfish, and that he trims off the top fin with scissors when suspending them beneath large popping-type floats with concave tops. The float creates noise when twitched on the surface. The commotion attracts big sea trout to the bait. A 1/4-ounce egg sinker replaces the small split shot on a large float rig when targeting trophy trout and the treble hook is upgraded to a No. 4 treble hook. One point of the hook is buried through both nostrils of the pinfish. Puppy trout will not bother this large bait. Therefore, anglers who are patient enough to wait for the strike of a bragging-sized trout and are not after just a cooler full of "keepers" can use this specialized bait.

To recap: live baits can be bought at tackle shops and piers or caught in cast nets. Minnows are caught by throwing a cast net on a surfacing school or by the use of a minnow trap. Pinfish are caught by hook-and-line around piers and jetties by using shrimp or cut fish for bait. Pinfish and shrimp can be caught also by using bait to attract and concentrate them, for catching with a cast net.

Fishmeal mixed with clay submerged in a tidal marsh attracts shrimp and small fish. Marked with a length of white plastic plumbing pipe stuck in the mud, the "shrimp ball" is covered with the cast net after a waiting period of about thirty minutes. Another method is to suspend canned-style cat food inside the toe of a nylon stocking in the water beneath a pier. A toss of the net under the improvised chum bag will produce shrimp attracted to the chum. This method will also produce pinfish - bait that a smart angler after truly big trout will toss into the live well and not reject over the side of the boat.

49

Vicky Rae Fredrick with a "chopper" bluefish caught near Wrightsville Beach.

The author with a 15-pound bluefish caught at Carolina Beach on a live menhaden.

Chapter 7

Bluefish Blowout Beats
Those Winter Blues

Justin was only seven years old. Up until then, his passion had been fishing for flounder. A tug on the line, a flopping fish in an ice chest and fried flounder after a day on the water were all that were needed to supply him with a day's worth of smiles that melted into his pillow at bedtime.

As with most anglers, Justin's transition from meat fisherman to game fisherman occurred unexpectedly when he accidentally hooked a fast and powerful torpedo of a fish.

We were flounder fishing in Snow's Cut, a channel of the Atlantic Intracoastal Waterway that forms the northern boundary of

51

Carolina Beach. The steep sides of "The Cut," which are blasted through solid limestone, form all sorts of structure that attracts many species of fish. A mud minnow hooked onto a "fish finder" rig enticed a strike. The rig consisted of a 1/2-ounce egg sinker threaded onto the line, a swivel, a 3/0 weedless Kahle hook and a 12-inch leader of 27-pound-test seven-strand wire.

Instead of the delicate thump of a flatfish, the strike of this fish was fast and vicious. Line streamed from Justin's light spinning reel at a rate that seemed, at first, to betray the surge of a red drum. However, this fish maintained its runaway pace against the maximum drag tension the 12-pound-test monofilament could withstand without snapping. In moments, the fish had stripped off most of the spool.

Line continued to melt from the reel as I frantically pulled up the anchor to give chase. A shrimp boat entered the narrow channel with her dripping nets hoisted overhead to help her speed home. As our johnboat drifted free, the rolling wake of the shrimper sloshed over the gunwales. I tried to wave the shrimper away from the taut line, but he never slacked off the throttle. He ran over the line just as the fish cleared the water on the opposite side of his boat.

Snatching the rod from my son, I plunged it deeply into the water until my shoulders were submerged. I spit out saltwater as the boat's wake splashed in my face. This maneuver kept the line from fouling in the shrimper's propellers. After the boat passed, I reeled the line tight again, and returned the rod to Justin. Switching on the bilge pump, I fired up the engine to pursue the fish.

A quarter of a mile later, we entered the Cape Fear River at the west end of Snow's Cut. The fish finally tired after its fourth run while Justin regained lost line.

As Justin's slender arms pumped the fish to the gunwale, it jumped twice and rattled its ice-pick teeth against the wire leader until they sounded like castanets. Justin was so startled at the sight that he nearly dropped the rod. He'd seen yearling bluefish before, but never one as gruesome looking as the full-grown sea monster gnashing its teeth on his leader.

I could say it was his guide's skill at coaching that helped Justin catch that fish, or that skill, rather than sheer luck, helped position the landing net under the fish as it ricocheted off the side of the boat like a basketball bank shot. But anyone who catches giant bluefish knows that they stay hooked once struck, unless their razor blade teeth miss the leader and clip the line.

Whooping in triumph, I hoisted the 15-pound "chopper" over the side. Justin dropped one of my best rods on the floor and jumped on a seat to protect his bare toes from the slashing teeth that sliced a gaping hole right through the tough plastic weave of the net and dumped the fish on the floor.

A bluefish that size is usually released, but this one was destined for home. Basted in butter and lemon juice over charcoal, his steaks tasted as fine to Justin as those from a king mackerel.

The years have advanced Justin's tastes in activities. Girls and team sports have incorporated themselves into his list of hobbies. Now, when I ask if he wants to go fishing, he replies, "That depends. Forget the flounder. Are the big blues running yet?"

No one knows for certain why bluefish have historically been reported by fishermen to disappear and reappear. The phenomenon was once thought to be the result of commercial fishing efforts. However, the National Marine Fisheries Service 18th Northeast Regional Stock Assessment Report concluded that, "Observed declines in recruitment could not be attributed to over-fishing."

Recruitment is the number of juvenile fish that survive on a seasonal basis once natural mortality and fishing mortality are taken into consideration. Scientists believe that there appears to be a problem with bluefish reproduction in recent years. Moreover, there is a good mix of older spawning fish up to age nine in the total population of bluefish, which indicates that over-fishing may not be the problem, according to Chris Moore, a senior fishery management specialist with Mid-Atlantic Fishery Council.

According to Moore, "The decline in the catch may be due to a decline in abundance, a decline in availability or a decline in angler preference."

This gives anglers a chance to reflect on past opportunities compared to present day opportunities for catching a variety of other fish. Whereas a decade ago, bluefish were the number one species sought by recreational anglers according to angler surveys, today striped bass are the most desirable species, thanks to successful recovery efforts for that species. There are also other species higher on the list of angler preference today. Therefore, bluefish have been relegated to an incidental catch rather than a targeted species.

Also, anglers release a greater number of bluefish, with nearly sixty percent of the catch set free. This makes it difficult to gauge the actual harvest on an annual basis.

Fishery managers have never accurately assessed the population of bluefish in the Atlantic Ocean. The annual commercial quota for bluefish by recreational anglers, based on averages over the previous three years, is set as a percentage of the harvest anticipated to be taken. Under this arrangement, the greater the recreational harvest the greater the commercial quota that is established. Since the commercial harvest gives the best picture of the health of the bluefish population and the commercial harvest is limited by a lower recreational harvest, the absence of high numbers of large bluefish reported by anglers along the coast of North Carolina during the late 1990's may be based upon perception and not fact.

Another answer may be in the biology of the fish, which is something of a mystery. According to Moore, "Bluefish as a species is hard to assess. They spawn along the continental shelf and migrate up and down the coast, and there is a relatively small commercial fishery compared to almost all other cash species. No large commercial fishery means a lack of data, such as provided by commercial fishermen who utilize more popular species such as king mackerel and flounder. We never know for certain if the bluefish population is up or down, just whether the catch is up or down."

Moore further explained that whereas anglers in one location along the coast report a bad season for bluefish, anglers at another location report good catches. The highly migratory nature of the species underscores the need for more information.

To stabilize bluefish numbers, a management plan for the fish was put into place in the early 1990's. The average number of citations for bluefish of at least seventeen pounds was also down from an average of sixty-six per year to fourteen in 1998. The last "good year" for catching bluefish was 1986, when landings totaled 115 million pounds. In 1996, the catch was nearly an all-time low of twenty-eight million pounds. Catches have been near the low mark since 1996, but may be slowly increasing.

The current management plan calls for a daily bag limit of ten fish of any size for recreational anglers. The scientific data in the stock assessment report indicate that to ensure recovery of the fish, the projected recreational limit should be one fish per day. However, since the data is questionable based on the limited commercial catch, the current recreational limit is being assessed and is apparently working.

So, does this mean that anglers should not go after bluefish? To the contrary, bluefish are still one of the most abundant game fish in coastal waters and begin arriving in the month of March. The appearance of the first schools feeding beneath diving gulls is enough to banish the winter "blues" from the soul of the winter-weary angler. The N.C. Division of Marine Fisheries upgraded the species' status from "depressed" to "recovering" in 1999. The management plan for the species seems to be helping to restore the species to historic levels and the reappearance of the big chopper blues along the best fishing areas of the coast will be welcome news.

The Cape Hatteras National Seashore is highly regarded by fishermen as the top spot in the world to catch bluefish. Bluefish are caught on trolling spoons just off the islands' beaches. Jerkbaits such as Got-cha plugs are the choice lures of fishermen. Trolling *Clark Spoons* and *Hopkins Spoons* around the Bonner Bridge as well as in the channel and along the outside bars of Hatteras Inlet is a very productive technique for catching bluefish.

Near Atlantic Beach, Cape Lookout Shoals, Beaufort Inlet, Fort Macon Inlet and the Fort Macon jetties are great locations for trolling or casting for bluefish from small boats. Fly-fishermen in the area use big nine-weight rods and lines to cast Clouser flies to schooling bluefish. Spinning rods are the most popular type of gear for casting bucktail jigs and spoons to surfacing schools. The best places for fishing are around the sandbars where flocks of birds diving on baitfish are the best indication that bluefish are feeding near the surface.

Fishermen in small boats also do well trolling and casting for bluefish inside Pamlico Sound and at Ocracoke Inlet. In the sound, there is an artificial reef at LORAN coordinates 27019.5, 40132.6 that holds lots of bluefish. Trolling with spoons works well at the reef. Anglers also cast surface poppers and spoons to catch fish near the surface. Just off Portsmouth Island the shipwreck of the *Midgette* attracts lots of bluefish.

Near Morehead City, trolling for bluefish east and west of Shackleford Banks and down to Cape Lookout is productive. From Cape Lookout Point out to two miles off the shoals is good territory. Barden, Beaufort, Morehead and Bogue inlets are also good spots. Fishermen should look for bluefish feeding on glass minnows in March and larger baitfish later in the year. Small topwater casting spoons and surface poppers are very effective when bluefish are feeding at the surface.

At Topsail Island, Topsail Inlet has always held good numbers of bluefish. However, the inlet is shallow and must be navigated with caution.

The best time to try to catch bluefish at Topsail Inlet is during the falling tide. Bluefish congregate on the south side of the inlet just offshore of the ocean breakers. Trolling Clark Spoons works well. However, if the fish are seen feeding in shallow water, drifting through the area while casting white bucktails is a good technique for catching them.

At Wrightsville Beach, the jetties at Masonboro Inlet are good places to catch bluefish on the end of the falling tide. Trolling spoons and casting jerkbaits, tinsel jigs, and floating plugs from a small boat are good techniques for catching bluefish at the jetties.

At Carolina Beach, bluefish can be caught almost anywhere. Anglers will find the mouth of the Cape Fear River, Corncake Inlet and Carolina Beach Inlet are good bets for bluefish on an outgoing tide. Cut baits and live baits such as mullet and menhaden fished on float rigs and on bottom rigs are popular choices in this area.

Just offshore of Kure Beach the Phillip Wolfe Reef (AR-378) and just offshore from Wrightsville Beach, the Meares Harris Reef (AR-370), probably offer the best chances along the coast for citation-sized fish of seventeen pounds. These fish are hooked on live baits, either caught in cast nets or from the bottom on gold-hook rigs, or on frozen cigar minnows. Fished on king mackerel live-bait rods and multiple hook rigs, these baits are attacked savagely by bluefish. Jigging with Hopkins, Stingsilver or Gibbs spoons is also very productive at these reefs as well as at Sheepshead Rock just off Corncake Inlet.

Near Southport, Jaybird Shoals at the western mouth of the Cape Fear River is a good place for casting surface lures from a boat. Trolling the area with spoons also produces fish.

Offshore of Long Beach, the Yaupon Reef and McGlammery Reef always hold bluefish in spring. Live mullet minnows and jerkbaits produce most of the bluefish on these reefs. Live baits are fished on float rigs with a wire leader and No. 4 treble hook set near the dorsal fin of the bait. If hooked in the lips, the bait is usually bitten off just behind the head and feeds the bluefish for "free." Jerkbaits like Got-cha plugs work best for sight-casting to feeding bluefish schools. Jigging spoons are also popular when the fish are deep and suspended over the bottom structure.

Justin Marsh with an Atlantic bonito caught on a tinsel jig.

Chapter 8

Bonito and False Albacore - What's in a Name?

Common names used to describe the same items vary from one region of the country to another. Unfortunately for saltwater fishermen, common names can lead to confusion when describing the many different species that anglers can encounter on any given day.

Saltwater fishermen's everyday names for the false albacore and Atlantic bonito are often interchanged across their range. These species are also collectively called "little tunny," "little tuna," "Boston mackerel" and "cerro mackerel." Atlantic bonito are also called "striped apes," while false albacore are also named "Fat Alberts" for their tenacious fighting abilities.

Perhaps the nicknames that best distinguish the two speedsters are "striped bonito" for the Atlantic bonito and "spotted bonito" for the false albacore. Horizontal black stripes on the steel-blue back and flanks identify a fish as the Atlantic bonito. Irregular black swirls mark the back and black spots dot the sides of the false albacore. These two fish can readily be told apart from one another, so fishermen across the Atlantic should be able to tell which species they're catching when bragging about a memorable trip to their friends.

Fortunately, scientists avoid all this confusion with common names by designating the Atlantic bonito *Sarda sarda* and the false albacore *Euthynnus alletteratus*.

But by any name these tiny tunas are some of the most fun to catch of all the saltwater species when hooked on light tackle.

For my purposes, I'll simply lump them together and call them both "bonito." Even though this may not be entirely correct, scientifically speaking, both of these fish put on such a spectacle of speed and power that the battle mimics in miniature the famed fighting abilities of their huge cousins - the giant bluefin, bigeye, and yellowfin tunas.

The presence of bonito within sight of land is news that spreads like a wildfire through the ranks of coastal small-boat anglers. Arriving just after bluefish make their appearance, the April run of bonito is anticipated as a rite of spring. Striped bonito and spotted bonito are always abundant, since neither is targeted by large commercial fisheries. Only bad weather can prevent fishermen from heading out to catch them. The main competition for these fish is among recreational anglers, with boats often cutting off one another when trying to jump-fish small schools that surface just long enough for a cast or two and disappear as quickly as they appear.

The Atlantic bonito tend to show up a little earlier than the false albacore because of temperature preference. Atlantic bonito like a temperature of 55 to 60 degrees, while false albacore prefer temperatures that range from 57 to 65 degrees. Both species can therefore be found in the brine at the same time and place and are often found mixing with schools of Spanish mackerel, which move in as the bonito action tapers off with the warming water temperatures of May.

Both species achieve weights of five to fifteen pounds. Their bodies are genetically adapted for high speed. Shaped like footballs, or according to scientific descriptions, the ideal "fusiform" shape, like the fuselage of a plane, these fish swim faster than any other of our small game fish. Their pectoral fins even tuck into folds, perfectly molded to the fins' contours, in the sides of their bodies, thereby creating zero drag while the fish is swimming. At first glance the tiny tails that power their runs simply don't look like enough propeller to get the job done. However, the entire body undulates to build up speeds that make monofilament fishing line sing as it cuts a wake across the surface when a bonito takes off.

Fishermen accustomed to catching other saltwater schooling species like bluefish, Spanish mackerel and king mackerel are simply not prepared to deal with the speed and endurance of bonito.

Justin Marsh with a false albacore caught on a trolling spoon.

While most of these other fish have blazing initial runs that strip line from fishing reels, bonito will make several such runs. Subsequent runs make the drag scream as loudly as the first before the fish has tired enough to be swung over the gunwale.

Finding the action is easy. Bonito feed on smaller fish like anchovies, silversides and glass minnows. Seabirds prefer the same diet. When bonito drive the baitfish to the surface, skimmers, pelicans and gulls start dive-bombing them from the air. From their high vantage, flying birds can spot action from miles away. All fishermen have to do is find the birds "working" the baitfish, and they will have found the place to fish.

Binoculars can be a big help when sight-fishing bonito schools. Not only does the magnification help fishermen to see the birds, but it also helps in determining whether the fish are actually surfacing. Birds can see to great depths beneath the water surface. Sometimes they will follow a school for miles before the fish come to the surface where anglers can catch them. Knowing for certain before rushing across several miles of ocean that the fish are on top where they are easier targets makes an angler's fishing time more productive.

On days when the birds don't show, or in the middle of the day when they are full from the morning's feeding frenzy, an angler can look for other boats that are in on the action. Another tactic is to look for birds resting on the water's surface. Gulls like to sit on the water in areas where they know baitfish are present, waiting for bonito to drive them to the top.

The trick to catching bonito is staying in front of the school. Whether streaking across the surface or appearing as a dark cloud beneath it, schooling bonito are constantly on the move. Paralleling the school, fishermen can cast ahead and then relocate the school after it sounds by continuing in the same direction the fish were heading.

A medium-action spinning rod is a good choice for catching surfacing bonito. Paired with a reel that holds at least 250 yards of 12-pound-test monofilament, the rod must have enough backbone to launch lures weighing as much as one ounce. Such heavy lures are needed to reach fast moving schools before they streak out of casting range or to allow long casts against the wind when necessary. The reel must also have a silky smooth drag system, since the smallest amount of extra friction from a stuttering drag while the fish is running can cause the line to break or the hook to pull loose.

Many anglers prefer larger reels. Their heavier weight is justified when a 15-pounder hits and the wind is blowing up a chop that prevents chasing the fish with the boat to regain line.

Another condition that can cause a reel "blowout" is a double or triple hookup. With several anglers fighting fish that have run in different directions, there is no way to follow one fish to regain line. Anglers often report bonito running off 300 yards of line before turning, and these fish are capable of making as many as five long runs.

When casting lures, a 12-inch, 30-pound monofilament leader or six inches of plastic-coated seven-strand wire leader prevents the razor-sharp teeth of the fish from cutting the line.

On calm days, many anglers use floating surface poppers to entice bonito, since these lures require little effort to keep them in the strike zone at which the fish are working. However, when the fish are scattered over large areas, lures such as bucktail jigs, tinsel jigs and heavy casting spoons are preferred for both their greater casting range and the fact that they allow the angler to make multiple casts rapidly.

Single-hook lures are preferred to those with treble hooks. Most bonito are released and a single hook does less damage to the fish than a treble hook. Besides, bonito are equipped with hard jaws, and a single hook is enough to hold them securely.

If the fish seem finicky, a drop of menhaden oil or a spray-on fish-scented attractant draws strikes on a seemingly "dead" lure. Switching to a smaller lure also can help. Bonito can be very size-selective of the lures they will strike.

When a bonito comes aboard, it has a nasty habit of ejecting great volumes of the baitfish it has been eating. Therefore, handling fish outside the boat is the best landing technique for fish destined for release. Swinging the fish directly into an open cooler will keep it from fouling the deck of a boat. Once the fish is in the cooler, the baitfish sprayed about inside can be observed. Matching lure size to the baitfish size will increase the number of strikes.

If a fish has yet to be caught, schooling fish can be observed closely and the size of baitfish they are chasing can be determined when the prey jumps clear of the water. Sometimes the baitfish may be a species normally "off the menu," like small menhaden. Bonito generally feed on anchovies, silversides and glass minnow. To draw the most strikes, it pays to know what the bonito are eating in order to match the lure to the baitfish.

When fly-fishing for bonito, most anglers use a floating line when casting to surfacing schools under calm conditions. However, intermediate-depth, weight-forward, sinking lines are necessary when the surface is choppy, since the fish have more difficulty in targeting lures presented on top. Strong winds require the use of fast-sinking lines. Eight to nine-foot rods with large capacity fly reels are preferred.

A smooth drag system is a must, as is an uncluttered casting deck. A stripping basket can be used to keep line tangles under control. Any loop in the line can result in a lost fish as a result of increased drag against the water. If the angler "palms" the reel or plays the fish by pinching the line in his fingers instead of using the reel drag, he must use a glove to prevent burning his fingers from line friction. The reel should be large enough to hold at least 200 yards of monofilament backing. The trick to catching bonito is staying in front of the school. Schooling bonito are constantly on the move, whether streaking across the surface or appearing as a dark cloud beneath it.

Fly-fishing leaders should be four to eight feet long, depending on water clarity. A longer leader is necessary in clearer water to fool bonito into striking a fly. A 12- to 20-pound tippet with a short wire or monofilament leader allows the angler to put a lot of pressure on the fish without the fish escaping with the fly embedded in its jaws.

Flies selected should imitate the minnows that the bonito are feeding on. Resin-bodied flies with artificial dressings are the most durable against bonito teeth. Many anglers also have good success with the tube-style flies usually used for salmon. Blue/white and chartreuse/white patterns of Clouser minnow flies closely imitate the anchovies and silversides that bonito prefer.

When the fish are really deep because of a cold rain, or during the middle of a sunny day when light penetration forces baitfish deeper, bonito can be found with an electronic depth finder. Once the mass of fish and baitfish is found on the screen, trolling reels such as those used for king mackerel and Spanish mackerel can be used to catch bonito. Large, big-lipped trolling lures that reach depths of twenty feet will catch lots of bonito.

When the fish prefer smaller lures, planers or downriggers are used to present spoons and jigs at the depths at which bonito are found on the depth finder. Lead trolling weights do not work well because they are sometimes mistaken for food by bonito. The fish will attack the lead, resulting in a cut line and the loss of weight, leader and lure, as well as any fish that may have happened to strike the lure.

Nets are preferred to gaffs for landing bonito. The fish lose unbelievable amounts of blood when struck with a gaff because a massive network of blood vessels is inherent in the fish to fuel their speed and stamina. Besides being unsightly and turning into a cleanup chore that stops the fishing action, fish blood on a deck makes it difficult for a fisherman to stay in a standing position in a rocking boat.

Patience is the key to landing a bonito. The tendency for a first-time angler is tightening the drag after an initial run or two. The result is a pulled hook, often at the expense of the fish's life, since the jawbone of the fish can be broken by its awesome power.

Four pounds of tension is plenty of drag for bonito. Novice anglers must not forget that drag increases as the line leaves the spool. Not only does less line on the reel increase drag as a consequence of the decreased diameter of the spool, the extra weight of the line in the water increases the pressure at the hook. Experienced anglers, especially when using fly-fishing tackle, loosen the drag when the fish is at its maximum distance from the boat — a wise tactic for anyone fighting with a long-running bonito hooked on spinning or bait-casting tackle. When fun fishing, an angler can increase the survival rate of released bonito by playing the fish to the boat as rapidly as possible, then using long-nosed pliers to shake the hook loose. Bonito expend such enormous amounts of energy that they will not survive if played to total exhaustion prior to release.

When the bonito action is hot, it is easy to overload the cooler with them. Most folks unfamiliar with bonito will not accept a gift of bonito fillets as readily as they will those taken from more popular food fish, so anglers must be careful not to retain fish they can't use immediately. The striped variety (Atlantic bonito) is edible when fresh. When cooked on the grill, the fillets taste very similar to offshore tuna. The skin should be left on the fillets to keep the soft flesh together when basting with butter and lemon juice or other sauces over the grill. Skinned and chunked, the meat can be deep-fried and served as fish nuggets. It also makes a great main ingredient for fresh tuna salad, and is delicious when smoked or canned. However, the oily flesh does not freeze well. Becoming soft when thawed, the meat is difficult to prepare and develops a strong flavor.

The spotted variety (false albacore) is considered inedible by anglers. However, the white belly meat is prized for making the "strip baits" preferred by offshore big-game fishermen. The silvery white belly meat is sliced along the horizontal axis of the body and a hook and leader sewn inside, forming a tube or plug style of natural-bait lure. Either variety of bonito can be used for this purpose, but the spotted bonito is considered to be the best bait for billfish. Bonito can also be used as whole "skip baits" when trolling for big-game fish. The entire fish is frozen in heavy brine to toughen the flesh and to preserve it for future use.

The most popular place to fish for Atlantic bonito is probably Wrightsville Beach, where the fish move to the AR-370 reef three miles offshore by April. Staying in the area for about three weeks, when their numbers peak they can be caught all the way inside to the beach.

False albacore make a strong showing in spring and fall off the Cape Lookout/Cape Hatteras area in what is becoming a world-class sport fishery. Many fly-fishing guides along the coast head for this area when the "Fat Alberts" arrive. Anglers can expect dazzling runs by dozens of fish per day at either location.

Justin Marsh caught this redfish by casting a lure underneath a dock in a tidal creek.

Red drum will strike a wide variety of lures that imitate minnows and shrimp.

Chapter 9

Sure-Fire Tactics For Catching Spring Redfish

Early spring is a tough time for inshore saltwater anglers. Water temperatures in estuaries seem too cold for the water to hold anything but an occasional speckled trout, so some old salts give up and migrate inland to join the freshwater guys casting for bass.

However, with a large dose of persistence, a little knowledge of where to look, and the same rod-and-reel combinations used to catch largemouth bass, dedicated saltwater anglers can tough it out and catch remarkable numbers of red drum weighing from two to six pounds.

As it does with freshwater bass, cold water packs lethargic redfish into deep holes, where they "attach" themselves to structure, including boat docks, channels, riprap banks and oyster beds. Once an angler finds these early spring redfish, he can catch them with the same types of tackle and lures he would select for catching largemouth bass in a lake.

Of course, it is a good idea to begin fishing with lures designed for saltwater use, because they'll hold up better during battles with surging spot-tails. The battle tactics must also be upgraded, because reflexes calibrated for largemouth are not sufficient for red drum. A largemouth bass angler will be caught off-guard by the power of a "channel bass" strike.

Knowing how redfish respond to chilly water temperatures is one of the keys to catching them. Heavy adult spawning redfish move offshore in winter, seeking water that is warmer than sixty degrees. They migrate far into the Atlantic to find their ideal comfort zone, then remain beyond the reach of anglers until inshore waters become warmer in spring.

While adult red drum can't tolerate temperatures below 50 degrees, juvenile "puppy drum" can handle cold water temperatures as low as 36 degrees. These younger fish are active between 50 degrees and 60 degrees, and tagging studies show that redfish up to six pounds seldom travel more than six miles from where they were spawned. This means that the one- to three-year-old fish are always available to inshore anglers.

Since these small fish don't migrate offshore, they must find the warmest areas of their territories during cold spells. When they find these refuges, they often congregate in huge numbers. Flounder giggers, for example, report seeing large schools of spring redfish resting on the bottom in deep holes in tidal creeks throughout the coast.

Another factor in finding red drum in early spring is salinity. Adult fish prefer high salinities of twenty to forty parts per thousand. This keeps them away from estuaries when spring floods that occur inland dilute the salinity in the mouths of coastal rivers.

In contrast, young redfish tolerate lower salinities, and they will even move into fresh water to find warm temperatures.

Though you can buy sophisticated meters for measuring temperature and salinity, they are unnecessary for the spring red-fisherman. All he needs is a thermometer on a string to test water temperature. If he wants to know the dividing line between freshwater and saltwater, just dipping a finger in the water and tasting it can provide all the information he needs.

Another key to finding redfish is water clarity. A "tide line," where clear saltwater meets the turbid fresh water discharge from an inland watercourse, usually occurs abruptly. The saltwater side is often the most productive for catching redfish, but it also pays to fish the freshwater side of a tide line, because temperature and salinity mixing cannot be determined from a boat deck. Mixing occurs and a tide line's location changes at different depths. The dividing line for temperature and salinity also changes constantly with the stage of the tide. Therefore, if fish suddenly stop biting, an angler can find them again by moving upstream on the incoming tide, or downstream on the falling tide to find the tide line.

Since baitfish are scarce in early spring, redfish feed mainly on shellfish. The same shrimp prized by human seafood lovers are equally relished by ravenous redfish, as are hard-shelled rock shrimp. However, catching a mess for bait with a cast net can be an exercise in futility, not to mention drenching the angler with cold salt spray. It is far more productive to use artificial lures that imitate shrimp and small baitfish for catching spring redfish.

To ensure success, an angler must target the places where redfish hunt for their prey, which is near structure such as boat docks. Whether they stand in saltwater rivers or freshwater lakes, boat docks are seldom far from deep channels. In tidal marshes, such channels often represent the only navigable water at low tide, not only for boats, but also for red drum.

Submerged in the water beneath the docks are generally found other manmade structure such as pilings, crab pots, sunken boats and other hard objects onto which oysters, barnacles and aquatic vegetation attach themselves. These objects create artificial reefs that attract shellfish and baitfish, which in turn attract redfish.

When fishing a dock with lures, it pays to try several different styles. Redfish are powerful fighters that can break monofilament lines with little effort by chafing them against sharp oyster shells embedded in the pilings. To avoid that problem, the angler must entice them from the outside of dock pilings with the first exploratory casts.

Minnow-imitating plugs designed specifically for saltwater such as MirrOlures and Yo-zuri minnows work well for this purpose. The styles without a lip don't catch flotsam, and they won't work the angler's arm to the point of fatigue in the swift currents of tidewater channels. Since red drum are bottom-feeders, it also pays to select lures that swim just above the bottom.

When an angler is unsure of the water depth, he can play it safe by using a slow-sinking lure. The rise and fall of the tide, as indicated by the barnacle line on dock pilings, may range from one to six feet, depending on the distance to the nearest inlet. The longer the distance from the nearest inlet, the less the tide changes. Fishing the same dock at different tide stages requires changing the depth of the lure presentation.

When testing unfamiliar waters, the use of an electronic depth finder can save lots of time. Since many docks along the coast have dredged access channels, a sonar unit helps pinpoint deep areas and shallow flats, allowing an angler to choose quickly between a shallow-running lure or a sinking lure when prospecting for fish at a dock. This spares the time that could be otherwise wasted by snagging lures on oyster beds or by waiting for an underweight plug to reach the bottom of a deep hole.

During low-water stages, fish leave their feeding areas in surrounding marshes and concentrate in the deeper water of navigable channels under docks, so the best time to fish a dock-lined channel is from the last two hours of falling tide to the first two hours of a rising tide.

If casting to the upstream, downstream and channel-facing sides of a dock doesn't draw a strike, the angler must boldly cast under the dock to pull lurking fish from inside their fortress.

There is no better lure for reaching under a dock to catch a red drum than a jig. Plastic tube skirts on leadhead jigs are super because they look and feel just like squid, a favorite entree for redfish. Weedless varieties of tube jigs are also available that lessen the odds of becoming snagged on structure. Tube jigs don't give a solid feel for bottom and structure like hard jigs. Therefore, most anglers prefer to use standard jig heads with plastic grub tails and natural hair jigs. When it comes to color, the most productive is white or a combination of red/white or pink/white because these are the colors that imitate shrimp.

To the artificial lure purist, tipping a jig hook with a bit of real shrimp or squirting a grub tail with a dose of shrimp-scented oil may seem unsporting, but it certainly increases the number of strikes from cold water red drum.

When probing for redfish under a dock by using a jig, most anglers position the boat upstream so the current carries the lure underneath the dock. However, it is a better idea to work from the downstream side first. The fish are more likely to be found on the downstream of a dock, because it requires less energy for them to suspend in the turbulence created behind the dock's pilings. When cast under a dock, a fast-sinking jig will travel downstream in an arc. A fish that follows the jig downstream will be more likely to strike outside the pilings, giving the angler a few precious seconds to turn the fish away from the pilings before it can wrap the line around them.

Fishing a dock from upstream is the last resort of experienced anglers. For this, smart anglers tend to avoid monofilament lines. Instead, they use heavy bait-casting rods with 30-pound-test superbraid lines to chunk jigs into the junkyards.

It is difficult to crank a reel handle to retrieve a jig with fingers crossed for good luck. But heaving a drum from underneath a dock even with superlines warrants any extra edge an angler can muster. Pound for pound, no largemouth bass can match a red drum for power and endurance. Without wasting energy on fancy acrobatics, a redfish will make several strong runs to try to gain the security of the dock piles before coming to the boat. More often than not, the line breaks off if a fish gets inside the rows of a dock's pilings. Conservation etiquette therefore demands the use of fast rusting wire hooks when jigging under docks for red drum.

Another type of manmade structure that draws spring spot-tails is a rock jetty or riprap seawall. Boulders placed to prevent erosion create habitat for redfish prey, and caverns in the stones provide redfish with a place to rest away from strong, scouring currents.

Red drum are present at rock walls during all tidal stages. However, the best time of day to fish a rock wall occurs just before low tide. It is even better if low tide occurs during a full moon or a new moon because these deep-water drum attractors hold fish that are driven from surrounding tidal flats and creeks by the lowest tides of the month. An astronomical low tide that occurs at sunset or sunrise creates a condition where an angler can catch redfish as fast as his lure slaps the water because that is when the fish prefer to feed. The action generally lasts only through the low tide period, then shuts off as redfish return to nearby marshes on the return flow of the tide.

For a beginner, fishing around rocks requires patience and an uncle who owns a tackle shop, because oyster-encrusted rocks have an insatiable appetite for lures — especially expensive ones. There are tricks, however, that help keep tackle-box casualties to a minimum.

A white bucktail jig, which can be fished "naked" or tipped with a grub, pork rind, shrimp, or strip of fish, is the best choice for fishing a rock structure in clear water. A yellow bucktail produces strikes better in stained water, but the design of the lure is more important than the color. The flat "butterbean" style, with the hook eye at the dorsal position, is best because the narrow profile allows the lure to slip through gaps in the stone. When stair-stepped down, it lies flat against rocks, keeping the hook point parallel to the stone to reduce or eliminate snags. Bending the hook point inward with pliers also helps, as does adding one foot of 30-pound-test plastic coated, seven-strand wire leader to protect against oyster shells cuts.

Wire leaders can be bought at tackle dealers, or they can be cut from a spool and attached to the bucktail and line by using a swivel and figure eight knots. Most fishermen make their own leaders because they are cheaper and can be tailored to the correct length. The shorter the leader can be to protect the line, the better, because red drum can be sensitive to the presence of metal near a jig. When red drum seem leader-shy, monofilament must be used to increase the number of strikes.

It pays to have jigs in several weights ranging from one-quarter ounce to one ounce, depending on the water depth and the velocity of the current. The weight should be just heavy enough for the jig to touch the stones on its descent without thumping firmly and creating a hang-up. Strikes usually come as the lure is falling, so keeping the line tight while raising and lowering the rod tip to hop the lure down the face of the rocks is important. Otherwise, the angler may not feel the strike in time to set the hook before the fish spits the jig out of its mouth. Strikes are most likely to come when the lure bounces off the last rock before hitting the bottom.

Another good tactic to prevent hang-ups in rocks is suspending the lure under a float. Redfish can be attracted to a lure or jig by chugging a concave-top popping cork the same way a bass fishermen pops a surface plug. Adjusting the depth of the float allows the lure to skim above the rocks. Cast up current, the rig drifts downstream. A long stretch of seawall can be fished on a single cast if the line is free-spooled from the reel. When a red drum strikes a jig on a float rig, the float simply disappears. If the line is in free-spool, the reel must be engaged quickly and the hook set as soon as line tightens.

Good lure choices for float fishing include jigs with plastic grubs and countdown types of minnow plugs. Rapidly sinking plugs tend to weigh down the float. If the sun is bright, grub tails with silver metal flakes or lures with silver flanks attract the most attention from red drum. On overcast days, good color combinations include gold, orange, red or hot pink.

Fly-fishermen also know that rock walls are good places to catch red drum. The trick is to fish at dead low or dead high tide, when the current is slack. Redfish lurk beneath flotsam and foam-accumulations in eddies between the rocks, and examine the mats of foam and debris for dead creatures that provide easy meals.

The Deceiver style of flies that ride point-up and poppers are best for catching red drum without snagging on rocks. Patterns with light color shades are best for fly-fishing. Brown, yellow, and gray work well where white foam is prevalent because dark colors create contrast that is seen more easily than light colors. Eight-weight tackle with a sinking-tip, weight-forward line is used to cast Deceivers. Heavy tippets allow flies to sink beneath floating trash without becoming cut off on rocks and shells. Red drum usually strike flies on the fall or during short, stripping retrieves. Poppers are fished on a floating line.

Since the limberness of a fly rod allows fish some leeway to escape into cover after the strike, the boat should not be anchored near rocks when fly-fishing. Allowing the boat to drift on the wind and current with the outboard idling, or using a trolling motor to keep the boat away from the rocks at the outer edge of casting range gives the angler a chance to maneuver a fish away. A steady pull perpendicular to the rocks under motor power gives the best chance of pressuring the fish away from a certain cut-off if he makes it into a cavern in the rocks lined with barnacles.

Another place for the fly-fisherman to find spring red drum is along the edges of grass beds in tidal marshes. As the sun warms the shallow waters of flats on a rising tide, redfish move from deep creek channels to feed and bask. Any high tide period is a good time to explore grass flats, but an overhead sun heats the water best in the middle of the day.

Hang-ups with flies can be frustrating. However, many weedless styles can be worked through the grass then drifted and twitched when it enters the current in open water. A fly fished in this manner imitates a minnow bursting from cover. Disoriented after being flushed into the open, such hapless prey is crushed by red drum before they can wriggle back into hiding.

Sometimes loud splashes in the grass or undulating movements in grass beds betray the presence of redfish. Presenting a fly when the fish are visible at the outside edge of grass beds will result in guaranteed strikes.

Grass beds are also the best type of cover for the ultra-light tackle enthusiast to test his skill and nerves. In-line spinners, Beetle Spins, weedless spoons, and tiny jigs with grubs like those used for catching freshwater crappie, draw strikes from cold saltwater redfish.

When using spider-web lines of less that six-pound test around grass beds, it is common sense to use a 12-inch monofilament leader of 12- to 20-pound-test line. The clear monofilament keeps the strike level high while preventing break-offs by grass stems. When using jigs with grubs, it is best to tie the leader directly to the line with a blood knot to keep metal in the water to a minimum. However, when using in-line spinners like the Rooster Tail and Mepps Comet, most anglers use a swivel between the leader and the line to prevent line twist.

Light-tackle anglers shouldn't become too complacent when boating three-pound puppy drum becomes routine. There are always a few 12-pound brutes prowling the grass beds in early spring to keep things exciting. Chaos in the cockpit often ensues as fishermen fall over one another while trying to hoist a snagged anchor or start an outboard motor as a bull red stretches someone's line and empties the reel. It's enough to warm an angler on the chilliest spring day. Indeed, a tight line and a screeching drag will make an inshore angler glad he stuck it out in the salt and left the bass fishing to the freshwater guys.

The author with a cobia caught on a live menhaden.

Chapter 10

Cobia Fun in the Summer Sun

It was the first of May, and king mackerel were reportedly hitting live menhaden around an artificial reef just outside Masonboro Inlet. The only way I could reach the kings was to venture into the ocean in my 16-foot, flat-bottomed johnboat. The forecast was windless, so I took a chance and went solo, freeing a pair of "pogies" — as local anglers call menhaden — from the live well to dance on the ends of king mackerel rigs.

Within two minutes, one of the menhaden baits enticed a dancing partner. Occupied with gaffing the king mackerel after a short battle, I didn't see the hulking silhouette that engulfed the other bait. The reel clicked a steady tempo quite unlike the urgent screech that telegraphs a king mackerel is on the line. Still, a hundred yards of line evaporated from the spool before I could ice the king mackerel, retrieve the bent rod and turn the outboard's tiller handle in pursuit. Yet another hundred yards melted from the reel before the fish paused in its first run.

Shark, I thought. But a shark's run is jerking and hesitant. This fish ran smoothly.

Amberjack, I guessed. The power was there, but unlike an amberjack, this fish stayed off the bottom and headed away from the structure of AR 370.

After fifteen minutes of battle at a sweat-drenching drag tension, I was sure I would see the fish. The surface boiled forty yards out, then the fish sounded. Hugging bottom against all the drag the 20-pound tackle could stand, the fish was still exerting tremendous power. After another fifteen minutes, it nonchalantly stripped off another 100 yards of line from the reel. The battle so far was a stalemate.

I eventually reeled the boat up to the fish, but the monster soundcd again. This time, however, he began to rise toward the surface under the pressure of the rod. Finally, the fish showed its side. *Cobia*! Unfortunately, all the gear I had onboard to boat him with was a tiny snake-king gaff.

Gaffed cobia are legendary for wrecking boats, gear, and fishermen! I was in a fragile johnboat. To make matters worse, a breeze began to ripple the water. Any chop would force me to cut the line and dash to the safety of the inlet.

The brute came alongside. The gaff struck. It straightened like a diaper pin! The fish ripped off 100 yards again and we were back to square one.

After reeling the boat back to the fish, I managed to retrieve a hand gaff I use for posing pictures from a storage compartment while holding the rod with one hand. Again and again, the cobia cruised within twenty feet of the gunwale. But whenever he sensed the boat, lazy sweeps of his powerful tail propelled him back to the bottom against all the drag tension the line could withstand without breaking.

After nearly three hours and a three-mile tow, I slipped the short gaff under the cobia's chin and wrestled him aboard. Dumping ice onto the deck, I upended the cooler over the cobia. It only covered two-thirds of the fish, so I sat on the cooler until he stopped thrashing.

Fortunately the weatherman's promise of calm weather held. I made it to the dock with only spray in my face and a sea monster aboard that weighed more than sixty pounds.

That's the way most anglers catch cobia — incidentally, while trolling for other species. Cobia are opportunistic feeders that take almost any bait, whether it is live fish, dead fish, shrimp, crabs, eels or artificial lures that imitate Nature's smorgasbord.

However, a growing number of anglers target cobia specifically, not only for their bad-to-the-bone fighting ability, but also for the flavor of their fillets.

Cobia start showing up when water temperatures warm to 65 degrees, but they'll continue to hang around in water is as hot as 80 degrees. Therefore, they're available to anglers from May until September.

May and June, however, is when they appear off the coast of North Carolina in large numbers. When tackle shops spread the word, "Cobia are here!" most offshore anglers stow heavy rods aboard in case they spot a shark-like shape that shows no characteristic dorsal fin while trailing their baits.

Finding the right structure is one key to engaging a cobia in battle. A buoy in an inlet or just outside an inlet is prime structure, especially when runoff-stained, food-laden water flows past on an outgoing tide. Cobia can be found circling or following any other large floating object. They are also fond of keeping company with rays, perhaps considering them another form of structure. Any school of rays is worth investigating for the presence of cobia.

Under calm conditions, cobia can be seen patrolling floating structure in search of a meal. Casting a jig tipped with a fish-belly strip is like throwing down a gauntlet in the face of a cobia. Rolling a streamer fly into the shadow of a buoy is a direct insult to his honor. If sight-casting to a cobia is not an option because of choppy or turbid conditions, they can be enticed by suspending a live mullet or eel on a king mackerel rig consisting of two No. 4 treble hooks tied to a wire leader under a balloon tied to the line. A strike will cause water pressure to burst the balloon, eliminating the resistance of a float while the fish is played.

When intentionally fishing for cobia, stout terminal tackle is mandatory. Plastic-coated, stranded wire and 3/0 to 6/0 hooks are preferred for anglers who use live bait and fish on the bottom. Fly fisherman must use heavy monofilament leaders to ensure success. The object is to select the strongest tackle that will not impair the action of the lure or bait.

Over-rigging for cobia is impossible since an average fish weighs thirty to sixty pounds. Anglers hook, but seldom land, larger cobia because they are usually targeting other species and aren't prepared for the size and endurance of a cobia.

Aside from possessing powerful muscles, a cobia has a palate of solid bone that can bend or break a 6/0 stainless steel hook under too much drag tension.

Cobia encircle a bait with their bodies when attacking. When "balling" the bait in this manner, a cobia almost appears to slap the bait into its mouth with its tail, which tends to wrap the leader around its tail. While the hook is imbedded in the mouth, the tail straightens. A light leader snaps. The fish swims free.

A cobia can also roll up in the line at anytime during a fight, breaking anything smaller than 40-pound-test monofilament by abrasion. Most cobia brought aboard actually have grooves cut into the head, gill plates or pectoral fins by the leader.

Some anglers use stout tackle suited for offshore bottom fish when fishing for cobia. They use a size 6/0 reel spooled with 60-pound-test monofilament or superbraid line for fishing deep channels, drop-offs and bridges in inshore waters. Heavy tackle is needed under these conditions because the pilings and rocks that attract cobia are usually fortified with razor-sharp oyster shells.

For prospecting channels, the best bait is blue crab. Cobia relish peeler or soft-shelled blue crabs, but they're expensive to buy and they attract non-target bait stealers. Hard-shell crabs also work. Breaking the crab in half, removing the legs and inserting the hook where the spike joins the body is the proper way to rig a crab bait. This technique provides two baits per crab, allows scent to disperse to attract cobia and prevents the hook from being set while the fish has only a claw in its mouth. It also minimizes resistance to current, allowing the use of the lightest sinker necessary to hold bottom.

A boat itself represents structure to a cobia, and the fish will strike bait right behind a rotating propeller. A hooked cobia and the shadow of a boat will also decoy others during a fight. In fact, earning a master's degree in cobia angling demands a crew successfully landing multiple hook-ups of the fish.

To catch fish following a boat or a hooked fish, a heavy spinning reel mated to a pier-fishing rod is kept at hand to cast a live bait or lure to the second fish. Since cobia slug it out near the boat after one or two initial runs, two fish can be played at once. The stronger fish is kept at a distance while the weakened fish is fought at the gun-wale. Swapping lines between anglers keeps them untangled. The motor remains running for maneuvering, but since the boat can't be navigated to both fish, the boat becomes a stationary fishing platform.

Although light gear allows many fish to escape, the biggest reason anglers lose cobia is from impatience. An angler who knows the exact breaking point of his tackle can expect a battle from an average sized cobia of at least forty-five minutes on standard, 20-pound class king mackerel gear. Anglers who attempt to force the fish to the boat will break the line or terminal tackle. Worse, they may gaff a "green" cobia if the gear holds. A green-gaffed cobia can demolish a fish box and destroy a couple of rods before flopping indignantly back over the side.

I prefer my cobia to be exhausted when coming aboard because even an aluminum ball bat will slip off their armored heads and dent a deck. For subduing a cobia on a deck, it is a good idea to use a rubber hammer.

Resembling a nightmarish cross between a shark and a mutant catfish, a cobia may be the ugliest saltwater game fish that swims. The beauty of a cobia is in the eating, and the final test of the fishermen comes at the cleaning table. Fillets are cut from the inside out to defeat the leathery, scaled skin. Then, with the skin side against the table, the knife is used to separate skin from flesh.

All red meat must be removed from the fillets. Otherwise, the fillets will have an aftertaste like sour milk. Besides paying attention to the lateral line area, all the red streaks that radiate from the lateral line at perpendicular angles must be removed. What remains of the meat after proper cleaning are two halved fillets that resemble four pearl-white pork tenderloins. Cutting these into six-inch lengths and baking, grilling or broiling them with lemon pepper or other seasonings results in a culinary delight.

A limit of Spanish mackerel caught on a tinsel jig.

Leslie Britt caught this five-pound Spanish mackerel by casting a lure from a kayak in the surf near Carolina Beach Inlet.

Chapter 11

Speaking Spanish

Like facets on liquid rubies, sea-breeze ripples flashed red sun-sparkles as we slipped out of Masonboro Inlet on a glorious morning in early May. The only sight more stirring to our souls than the breaking of dawn was the vision of sea birds wheeling against the hot pink sky. Dive-bombing for breakfast into acres of baitfish, the dozens of gulls and terns showed us the location of a hungry school of Spanish mackerel.

My wife, Carol, and son, Justin, quickly went into action. An ice chest was maneuvered to the back of our 19-foot Jones Brothers

Bateau. A pair of king mackerel live-bait rods rigged with Penn No. 9 reels was placed into the transom rod holders. Each of my mates manned a reel, letting out 100 feet of line tied to a Clark Spoon held just below the surface by a two-ounce trolling sinker.

As we slowly circled the edge of a panicked school of glass minnows, we saw dozens of Spanish mackerel slash through them and become airborne, leaping above the surface right beside the boat. The warning clicker on Justin's fishing reel screeched. Before he could lift the rod from the holder, Carol's reel also cried, "Fish on!"

Keeping the motor in gear, I kicked the ice chest lid open with a toe while keeping my hands on the steering wheel and throttle. Lifted from the water but still fighting the hook in the air, Justin's fish quickly hit the ice and was immediately followed by Carol's. Pulling the leaders taut and closing the lid until only the jaws of the fish protruded from opposite corners of the ice chest, the two anglers quickly worked the spoons free with needle-nosed pliers and cast them back over the transom.

The action was non-stop after that — not another rod made it back into a holder without having a fish attack its trailing spoon. Within minutes, other boats witnessed our luck and got in on the action. All the extra boat traffic running through the school eventually spooked the fish and they sounded into the emerald depths of the Atlantic. If the other boats had only worked the edge of the school as we did instead of running through the center, the fish would have stayed on top for at least another hour.

Fortunately, we were finished with the school, having caught a limit of ten Spanish mackerel apiece. While others trolled, we headed back through the inlet to cast in tidal creeks for red drum. The sun had climbed just high enough to yawn from pink to orange. The bottom of its chin had yet to clear the horizon.

Such fantastic fishing trips would seem to some anglers a matter of luck. However, anyone can catch a limit of Spanish mackerel if they prepare for the occasion and know when and where to look for fish. One of the best sources of information about Spanish mackerel is Tex Grissom, owner of *Tex's Tackle* in Wrightsville Beach. It was

Grissom who had told me how to catch the fish the day before our trip.

"Spanish mackerel show up near the inlets by mid-April, but the best fishing starts in May," said Grissom. "When the water temperature climbs to between 65 and 68 degrees, a run of fish shows up that can average four pounds apiece. After a couple of weeks the size of the fish declines to one to two pounds each. However, Spanish mackerel school according to size, and anglers can move to another location if the school they are fishing is made up of small fish."

Although Spanish mackerel are found all along the state's coastline, the inlets of southeastern North Carolina offer some of the best Spanish mackerel fishing to be found anywhere. As tasty on the table as they are fun to catch, Spanish are the fish of choice when a quick "mess of fish for supper," is the objective of a day on the water.

The easiest way to catch Spanish mackerel is by trolling a Clark Spoon. Grissom prefers No. 0 and 00 sizes because they imitate the small baitfish that Spanish mackerel eat. He prefers silver spoons, although he said gold spoons sometimes produce better on cloudy days. Spanish can be very selective of the size of baits they hit. If they don't hit an initial offering but are seen jumping all around the boat, it's a good idea to go to a smaller size lure.

"The most important thing when trolling Clark Spoons is to get the boat speed right," said Grissom. "Most fishermen troll too slow to obtain the correct action from the spoon. A minimum speed of four to five knots is the speed for catching Spanish."

When Spanish mackerel are really biting, fishing one rod per angler is enough. Trolling with more rods results in tangles and lost fish because schools of fish are so thick that all lures trolled will hook a fish.

"I only fish two rods when I am after Spanish," said Grissom. "I use a number one planer on one side of the boat, which will take the spoon down seventeen to twenty feet deep. On the other side, I use a one or two-ounce trolling sinker with a bead chain swivel. A chain swivel or ball bearing swivel is a necessity when trolling spoons because they can twist the line badly. The trolling sinker takes the lure down to five feet or so below the surface. The depth the spoons will reach is dictated by line length. One hundred feet of line will take the lures to their full depth. With the planer, that can be deep enough to hit bottom near the beach. In that case, you should let out less line."

While most anglers simply troll for Spanish mackerel by using their king mackerel live-bait rods, some carry hand-lines, ready-rigged when surfacing fish are spotted. Hand-lines are rigged with a soft line like parachute cord because it is easy on the hands when hauling in a big fish. Spanish mackerel can easily reach seven pounds in weight and the occasional big king mackerel will also strike a Clark Spoon.

Hand-lines are wrapped around a board or plastic depth marker. The line is tied directly to a planer or trolling weight. A leader is tied to the planer or trolling weight and a spoon tied to the leader.

"The leader can be the most important part of Spanish fishing," said Grissom. "It pays to use the smallest diameter leader you can get away with. I use 25- to 30-pound test monofilament. When the fish are finicky, I drop down to a 20-pound leader or use a fluorocarbon leader that is less visible to the fish. However, fish will bite through the 20-pound leader after only a few are boated, so you have to check it for wear. The leader should also be at least fifteen feet long. The longer the leader, the more strikes there will be on the spoon because sometimes the fish are really shy of a planer or weight."

Early and late in the day are the best times for catching Spanish mackerel. The decreased light penetration brings baitfish and the Spanish mackerel that eat them to the surface as well as making lines, leaders, and gear less visible to the fish.

Weather does not seem to be much of a factor. If it is calm enough to be out on the water, it is a good day to catch Spanish mackerel. However, the wind can stack baitfish against structure and even blow them inside inlets. For example, on a north wind, the north face of the north Masonboro Inlet jetty will be loaded with Spanish, while on a south wind the south face of the south jetty will be a hotspot.

"If the boat traffic is light, I begin trolling inside the jetties," said Grissom. "Then I watch for birds or surface-feeding fish. Depending on the wind, I will turn and go out around either jetty. Another thing to watch for is the line that forms on falling tide just outside the inlet. The inside of the tide line is usually cloudy and the outside is clear. Spanish will usually be on the clear side of the tide line."

The Meares Harris Reef (AR-370) is also a top destination for spring Spanish. Located just 3.5 miles from Masonboro Inlet, "The Tug" and "Liberty Ship" attract hundreds of boats seeking fish on balmy weekend days. It is not unusual to see anglers in aluminum johnboats catching limits of fish there when the wind is calm.

"When it is too crowded to troll, I like to cast to surfacing schools with a spinning rod," said Grissom. "Sometimes you run across a school right inside the Intracoastal Waterway near an inlet where there is not enough room to turn the boat around to troll. That's when you can really have some fun."

Using a medium-action rod, Grissom casts lures on 8-pound test monofilament. Got-chas in all white or red-head/white-body, yellow-head/white-body are great for catching Spanish, according to Grissom. He said the gold-hook models seem to have the flash that attracts more strikes than the silver-hook models. Other lures that work well are the Yo-Zuri minnow in black-back/silver-body and green king mackerel patterns. When there is enough wind to make casting difficult, Kastmaster Spoons can be used due to their streamlined shape as can white bucktail jigs. For anglers who want to double their fun, a standard two-jig speckled trout rig often results in double hook-ups, according to Grissom.

Captain Lee Parsons of *Gottafly Guide Service* in Wrightsville Beach takes clients out for Spanish mackerel with a focus on light tackle and fly-fishing. When fly-fishing, he likes to drift over an area where fish are surfacing. Once he drifts away from the fish, he motors upwind again and drifts back over the school.

"I let the boat drift and have my angler do roll casts," said Parsons. "I have him let out thirty feet of line and sweep the rod really slow to imitate the glass minnows Spanish like to eat. By letting the fly drift along, the angler gets to see lots of exciting strikes within fifteen feet of the boat."

Parsons uses an 8-weight rod with a floating or intermediate line. While fluorocarbon may draw more strikes, he said that if it knots up ahead of the fly, the knots are shiny enough that Spanish mackerel will strike them, cutting the leader.

"I generally use a 12-pound mono leader," said Parsons. "I tie a Crystal Flash Clouser on a long-shank hook, usually a No. 1 or 1/0 Mustad 34011. The long shank protects the leader. Also, the small diameter leader slides between teeth like dental floss if the fish is hooked deep. Larger leaders will be snipped off by the bite of a Spanish."

Parsons also uses light spinning tackle to troll for Spanish. The light tackle gives more thrills in fighting the fish than heavy trolling gear.

"When trolling with spinning rods, I use a rod-length of 20-pound fluorocarbon leader and attach the leader to the line with a ball-bearing swivel. By trolling a No. 00 Clark Spoon at six to eight knots, I catch lots of Spanish. The lure alternately skips the top of the water and then dives at that speed. The action really turns the fish on. Without the swivel, the line would twist badly."

Parsons sets two rods in the back of the boat and uses flat-line clips at the transom to keep the spoons at the water surface. He trolls one spoon fifty feet behind the boat and another at seventy-five feet back. From a center rod holder, he trolls a third line that is let out 150 to 200 feet with no flat-line clip. The distance differential between the lines allows sharp turns without the lines tangling with one another. The long line picks up fish the flat-lines miss.

"If I am not getting any action on top, I turn the boat into the wind and kill the throttle to let the lures sink. This will often catch fish that are deep," said Parsons.

Steve Laughinghouse compares his 10.8 pound "doormat" to Vinnie Tomaselli's two very nice "keepers" caught while power drifting an inlet.

Chapter 12

Power-Drifting for Flounder

The sun had just begun to show its face above the mirror of the Atlantic. Wayne Cook was my fishing partner on that long-ago day and we had already caught twenty flounder of various sizes. That was in the days preceding size limits for the species and when a busy weekend day saw perhaps five other boats drifting with the current in Carolina Beach Inlet trying to catch the main ingredient for a fried flounder dinner.

One other boat had arrived before us. It was there in the darkness when we dropped our first baits over the side. A true old-timer captained the brown, aluminum boat with a V-bottom and the steering wheel in the bow. Secretive as a mink, he led flatfish to his net on the opposite side of the boat from us so we couldn't see what he was using for bait or how he tied his rigs. But he always seemed to be hooked up to a fish and was out-catching the two of us by a ratio of three fish to one.

Making exactly the same drifts, or so we thought, we shadowed the "old man in the brown boat" to see if that would increase our catch. But his success, relative to ours, remained the same.

Frustrated, I finally managed to time a drift to coincide with the old man's. Once we were gunwale to gunwale, I asked him how he was doing.

"Only have about sixty," he said. "Did a lot better yesterday."

He hooked another flounder and played it to the net. This time we were close enough to see his rig even though he tried to hide it as he scooped the fish over the opposite side.

While he unhooked the fish, I told him how many we had.

"You fellows would do better if you left the motor running instead of shutting her off. That way you could stay along the edge of this bar where the fish are laying."

That was all he would say. He wasn't much at sharing secrets with the competition. But that tip has resulted in more flounder for me over the years while drifting inlets than any other. The old man had left his motor running and used it to make subtle changes in his drift pattern to keep the bait in productive areas instead of leaving the boat's direction to the mercy of the tide and wind.

The key to drift-fishing success is that after a productive area is identified by catching fish, the exact area must be hit again during subsequent drifts. That is a difficult achievement without using the motor for maneuvering. Each time an angler motors up current and sets out his baits on the bottom, the tide's direction and velocity changes. The wind plays its hand as well in pushing the boat off course.

By using the motor to steer the boat, the same drift pattern can be repeated many times. It can also be used to slow the speed of the boat once it is over a productive bottom. This keeps the bait in the strike zone longer for catching more fish. It also results in larger fish. Big flounder are lazy and will not chase a bait far. They hit most often when the bait is still and not being dragged at a speed of three knots.

Power-drifting also allows the inevitable snagged rigs to be pulled free quickly. There is no waiting to start the motor before stopping the boat, or taking up other baits. Being able to quickly motor back in the direction of the drift allows snagged rigs to be pulled free, which results in fewer lost rigs, less re-ties and more fishing time.

Most of the time, there are ledges or bars in an inlet that run perpendicular to the current. The downstream sides of these ledges hold the most flounder. Flounder wait for the current to carry baitfish across the ledge and ambush them as they swim overhead.

Under power, a boat can be used to keep baits along the downstream side of a ledge where the flounder are waiting. The bow of the boat is pointed into the current and the motor bumped in and out of gear to keep the baits in the strike zone. The pattern is a zigzag, with the baits dragged to the top of the ledge, then allowed to drift with the current to the downstream side. Generally, the strikes come just after the bait rolls off the crest of the ledge, but the longer and more subtle the grade of the drop-off, the wider the area that holds fish.

When power-drifting, it takes a rig with more weight to stay on the bottom than is generally used when drifting at the speed of the current. The rig the old man used was not an over-the-counter "flounder and fluke rig," but used a three-way swivel to separate a dropper hook from a sinker, keeping the bait swimming off the bottom.

The weight of his power-drifting rig is a two- to five-ounce torpedo sinker. The size depends on the water depth and current speed and must be adequate to maintain constant contact with the bottom. A three-way swivel is tied to the line. The sinker is tied to the three-way swivel with 18 inches of 20-pound test monofilament leader. A 2/0 Kahle-style hook or wide bend hook is tied to the swivel with 24 inches of 20-pound test mono. This is a good starter rig. However, the lengths of both leaders can be adjusted as conditions require, as well as substituting lighter line for the leader with the hook when hang-ups are common. The lighter line will break, losing only the hook. It is easier and less expensive to tie on a new hook than a new sinker and swivel after a break-off.

Deedee Harris caught this flounder by casting a bucktail jig to the edge of an oyster bed in the Lockwood's Folly River.

The spring weed-guard on this hook kept the bait from snagging in the edge of the grass bed that held this flounder.

Chapter 13

Get the Edge on Carolina Flounder

When the water temperature heats up in late June, flounder action at the inlets begins to cool down. Anglers tired of the monotony of drifting inlets for diminishing numbers of flounder among increasing numbers of water scooters can find excitement along the edges of grass beds and navigation channels.

Flounder prefer water temperatures in the 70- to 75-degree range. Once the seawater temperature rises above this level, flounder seek cooler temperatures in tidal creeks and navigation channels. Hungry flounder hide along the edges of grass beds, waiting to ambush baitfish that dart in and out using the grass for escape cover. Forced from hiding as the high tide ebbs, minnows and fry concen-

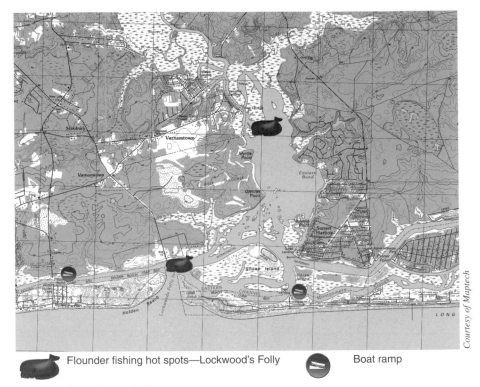

Flounder fishing hot spots—Lockwood's Folly   Boat ramp

Courtesy of Maptech

trate at the edge of the grass.

Grass beds marking drop-offs at the edges of creek beds or navigation channels offer the most productive fishing. Likely spots can be found just around the corner from any inlet. There is virtually nowhere along the Carolina Coast where this type of cover cannot be found. Schools of menhaden or finger mullet traveling around a point at the edge of a channel are a good indication that flounder lie below.

In Southport, North Carolina, flounder fishing is an art nurtured to its highest form. Several guides specializing in skinny-water fishing target trophy flounder in that area of the state. One of the best is guide Captain David Mammay, who lives in Long Beach and operates *Reel Success Guide Fishing Service.* Mammay has guided fishermen to uncountable, citation-sized flounder of over five pounds. He has developed techniques and opinions specific to his home waters that are applicable to flounder fishing anywhere. When we

fished together, he cast over and over to a spot no bigger than a basketball hoop in one of the creeks just west of Southport.

"I've caught really nice flounder on that little point of marsh
grass," he said. "If you catch a big fish in a certain spot, there may
be another right beside it. The same spot will also give up another
big fish on another day."

Knowing such tiny areas that hold huge monsters, like the seven-
pounder Mammay caught in the same spot a dozen casts later, is one
key to success. An angler usually finds those places only by making
lots of casts. Mammay finds his fishing holes by targeting areas that
have certain characteristics.

"I look for structure, bait and deepwater access nearby," said
Mammay. "I work points and grass bed edges where bait is schooling, and oyster beds and piers lining the edges of creek channels. I
try to find manmade food sources, such as commercial fish and crab
cleaning houses along the edge of the Intracoastal Waterway that
dump readymade chum down chutes into the water. Where such an
operation has underlying structure, such as old pilings, sunken boats
or piles of shells alongside a navigation channel, there will be bragging-sized flounder feeding.

"To illustrate how well a food source attracts big flounder, I once
saw a pair of hunters cleaning some marsh hens on a dock. I fished
there the next day and caught a 10-pound flounder. When I cleaned
it, it had marsh hen feet inside its stomach."

The boat should be anchored forty feet from the edge where
minnows are seen swimming. If a steep drop-off is present or strong
tides roll the fisherman's sinker away from the grass at more than a
gentle bounce, the boat should be moved closer, creating less resistance by shortening the amount of fishing line exposed to the current. The best method for fishing edges involves fan casting, the
same technique used while fishing for largemouth bass with a plastic
worm along the shoreline of a lake. When using a live minnow, the
bait is cast into an upstream pocket in the grass, then left to soak for
a few minutes. It is then worked back to the boat by alternately raising the rod tip, then lowering it to allow the bait to fall back on a

tight line. A turn of the reel handle is all that is necessary to take up slack on the fall. The "bump-bump" of flounder mouthing the bait is subtle. Therefore, it is imperative to maintain a tight line to "feel" the bait at all times.

"Light tackle brings more strikes than heavy tackle," said Mammay. "I use 14-pound-test, low-stretch monofilament with a 14-pound-test leader. I attach the leader to the line with a No. 8 swivel and slide a one-ounce egg sinker onto the line above the swivel. The hook is a 2/0 Kahle hook. I consider this to be a heavy hook, but I have had big flounder straighten even the 2/0."

After the bait is worked to the boat, it is presented again about two feet downstream from the previous cast, then worked back again in the same fashion. After an area has been thoroughly covered, the anchor is raised and the boat allowed to drift with the current along the edge of the grass and re-anchored. New water can then be fished with a minimum of effort.

The best tide stages to catch flounder are two hours before and after the high tide, according to Mammay. However, he does have areas that produce well on lower water. Once he finds the water depth the fish prefer, he works the baits at that same depth in nearby areas. He continues to fish at the preferred water depth as the tide moves up or down by moving the boat closer or farther from the bank.

For fishing dirty water, Mammay uses a 6- to 8-inch leader to keep the bait close to the bottom. In clear water, he uses a 12- to 14-inch leader, since a bottom-hugging fish can see the bait swimming above it at a greater distance. When he feels a flounder strike with his highly sensitive, graphite bait-casting rod, he lets the fish chew on the minnow for a while.

"A flounder will scale a mullet with his teeth, so I wait longer before setting the hook so he can swallow the bait when I'm using a mullet for bait. With a menhaden, he'll suck it right down. If he lies there and doesn't move away, I lift the sinker off the bottom to make him mad. When he begins to move, I stick him. If he swims off as soon as he hits, I let him go until he stops. He will not go far. When

I set the hook, I hit him hard enough to send him to the dentist."

Phil Pare, a sport fisherman who fishes the edges of Snow's Cut and the Cape Fear River and the docks lining the edge of the Atlantic Intracoastal Waterway between Wrightsville Beach and Carolina Beach, showed me a way to avoid hang-ups when fishing live bait around structure. A standard Kahle hook was once my hook of choice, but hang-ups were common due to shell beds, stumps and casts that landed inches inside, rather than inches outside, the edges of grass beds.

Pare had me fooled for some time with what I believed was his superior casting ability since he never hung his hook in the grass. But in the process of netting yet another flopping flatfish for him, I noticed that he was using a bass worm hook with a wire weed deflector. That being a freshwater hook and my having only a salt-water tackle box onboard presented a problem. Luckily Pare had some extra hooks and let me try them. Weedless hooks are also available in the Kahle design, also called "flounder and fluke" hooks by manufacturers. Now I never leave home to try fishing for flounder at the edges of structure without them.

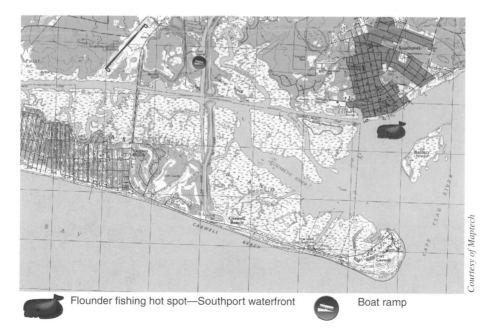

Courtesy of Maptech

Flounder fishing hot spot—Southport waterfront   Boat ramp

Chris Robbins with his North Carolina state record and IGFA youth world record sheepshead.

Chapter 14

Sheepshead Records Shattered by Twelve-Year-Old

At the ripe old age of twelve, Chris Robbins has caught numerous species of fish that run in size from tiny pinfish to huge yellowfin tuna. However, all of those previous fish were eclipsed on June 14, 1999, when Robbins hooked and landed the fish of a lifetime at the Bonner Bridge at Oregon Inlet. That fish was a spectacular sheepshead weighing nineteen pounds, four ounces. The huge fish not only became the new North Carolina state record sheepshead, it also became the International Game Fish Association (IGFA) world record for the species in the youth fisherman category.

David Robbins was disappointed that he had to work, while his son, Chris, traveled from their home in Franklinton, North Carolina to the coast to spend some vacation time. Chris was staying with his grandparents and he was overjoyed to find out that his uncle, Jerry Robbins, was going to take a week off to fish Oregon Inlet, and was going to invite him along.

"We went to Oregon Inlet because the wind was blowing too hard to fish anywhere else," said Chris. "We were fishing out of a 17-foot boat. We tied up to a bridge piling right at the draw section. The channel there has thirty feet of water. My uncle was untangling some stuff and I was just reeling in my line. I thought the hook was hung. But when I felt the fish, I hollered for Jerry to get the net!"

Chris was using fresh shrimp for bait because they were fishing for black drum. He was using a stiff boat rod and an old level-wind reel spooled with 50-pound test superbraid line and a 2/0 wide bend hook tied onto a homemade 40-pound-test bottom rig. Jerry thought for certain that the fish was a black drum until he got a look at the teeth.

"Jerry like to have went crazy when he saw the fish," said Chris.

"He was so big we had to double him up to get him inside a 72-quart cooler. He was twenty-nine inches long and twenty-six inches around."

When they returned to the boat ramp, a North Carolina Division of Marine Fisheries (NCDMF) survey official checked the fish. It was large enough that he decided to weigh it on his hand scale. He became extremely excited when he checked his files and told Chris that he may have a state record fish. At his suggestion, Chris and his uncle took the fish to the Oregon Inlet Fishing Center where it weighed 19 pounds on commercial scales. They then carried the fish to *Whalebone Tackle* in Nag's Head to make certain the fish was correctly weighed on certified scales for entry into the NCDMF salt-water tournament.

"The superbraid line was the key to catching that fish," said Chris. "He wrapped the line around the bridge piling four or five times. Any other line would probably have been cut."

In 1982 Everett Richardson caught the previous state record sheepshead at Carolina Beach. That fish weighed eighteen pounds, seven ounces.

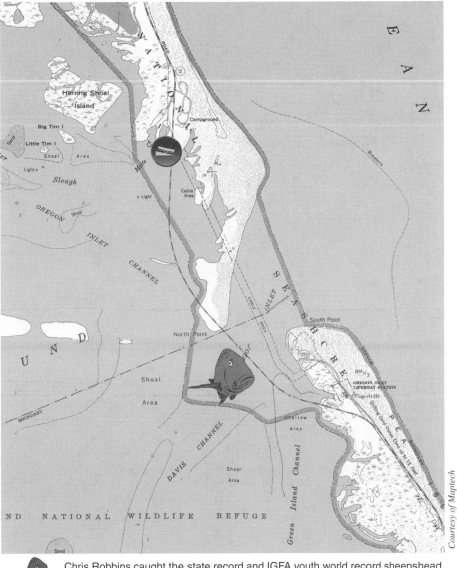

Courtesy of Maptech

 Chris Robbins caught the state record and IGFA youth world record sheepshead at the Oregon Inlet Bridge.　　Boat Ramp

Captain Jimmy Price with a big speckled trout caught on one of his "Trout Killer" jigs near Southport.

Chapter 15

Speckled Trout Worth the Price

Fishing for spotted sea trout can be a maddening addiction. The here-today, gone-tomorrow habits of this highly prized game fish make few anglers experts at consistently taking home the main ingredient of a trout dinner, let alone a four-pound citation sized speck for bragging rights.

The biggest certified specimen of these gorgeous, delicately flavored fish that has been taken from North Carolina waters was caught at Wrightsville Beach in 1961 by John R. Kenyon and weighed a whopping twelve pounds, four ounces.

Not far down below Wrightsville Beach along the Cape Fear River is a fishing guide in Southport who is without peer when it comes to "speckled trout," as he calls one of his favorite species. There is a lot of competition among guides at the mouth of the Cape Fear River. Therefore, there is always some argument over which guide is the best flounder fisherman. However, all Southport fishing guides agree as to exactly who is "Mr. Trout." Southport guide, Captain David Mammay, said, "If you want to catch speckled trout, Captain Jimmy Price is the best."

To get the angle on hot-weather speckled trout, I called Price and arranged a trip. As we left the N.C. Wildlife Resources Commission access area at Wildlife Creek in Price's 18-foot Boston Whaler one blustery summer day, Jimmy acknowledged that a monster such as Kenyon's fish is rare, indeed.

"I have caught several specks that weighed over nine pounds, but a ten-pound trout is the fish of a lifetime. But I'm sure that there are record fish all along this area," said Price.

Most folks think of winter as the prime season for speckled trout. However, Price says the fish are located in the area between Southport and Bald Head Island all year. They are also present in most of the sounds and coastal river system throughout the state.

"Speckled trout start biting when the water hits fifty-eight

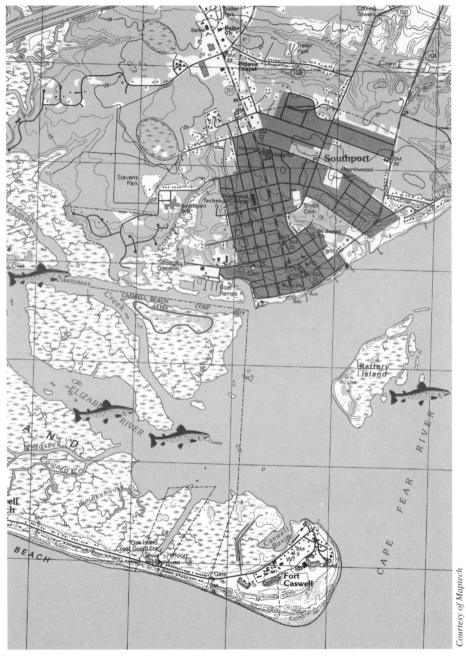

Speckled trout hot spots—Southport.

degrees, with seventy degrees being the ideal temperature. However, I have never seen it too hot to catch specks. In winter we catch bigger fish, but they are fewer and farther between. In summer, we catch more fish, but they mostly weigh one or two pounds, along with the occasional big fish of up to five pounds," said Price.

Price explained several things that helped unravel the fickleness of specks for summer anglers as we began trolling the oyster beds at the mouth of Dutchman's Creek.

"Most fishermen have never heard of trolling for trout," said Price. "But it is one of the fastest ways to find the fish. You can troll a MirrOlure or jig-and-grub along the edge of a grass bed adjacent to good trout structure, like an oyster bed or a drop-off. Once you find the place where the trout are holding by catching a fish, you can usually anchor the boat and cast to the spot and catch fish. It doesn't always work because sometimes they won't hit anything but the trolled bait. They can also be so picky that they only want a specific lure and they want it trolled only from one direction."

Price used standard curly-tailed grubs on lead-head jigs for casting and trolling for years, then switched to a Fin-S grub. In spite of the better luck he had with the Fin-S, he found that the forked tail had little action when the lure was retrieved slowly, the way summer trout like it.

"We also had good luck with Sassy Shads, because they had better action at slower speeds. I didn't like the action of the Fin-S as it was slowed just when it was coming to the boat. A lot of fish will hit right at the boat, so I figured that I could get in some extra fishing time on each cast with a lure that had more action. I cut off the flat, Sassy Shad tail and glued it on to replace a cut-off Fin-S tail. It worked really well. Sea Striker has just come out with the lure commercially, called the Trout Killer," said Price.

The fish usually strike lures trolled along the bank side of the boat, so Price fished two rods on that side, then switched them to the bank side again when the boat was turned around to make another pass. After trolling a few minutes with no luck, we anchored the boat and cast MirrOlures to no avail.

"It is hard to catch them on an east wind like this one or on a northeast wind," Price said. "Chalk it up to the fickleness of the fish. I caught ten specks right here two days ago."

Price had tied on three different colors of grubs and had dipped the tails in four different flavor/color combinations of DipNGlo scent, including greens and reds scented with shrimp or garlic.

"They really like the garlic scent, but you never know what they will hit on a given day," said Price.

Reeling in the lines, we tried several oyster beds along the Elizabeth River, where we still had no luck. Then we headed west to the Cape Fear River, where numerous sloughs and creeks provide the combination of deep and shallow water that speckled trout call home during the summer.

"If it was nearer the full moon, we could fish at night," said Price as we motored carefully through a channel lined with oysters behind Battery Island. "As the week before the full moon progresses, trout bite less and less during the day. Then, when the full moon comes up, you can hear and see them striking on top, hitting minnows and shrimp in the creeks like Dutchman's and Molasses. You can catch them on Jitterbugs, Devil's Horses, Torpedoes, and Nightstalker (black) or Purple Demon MirrOlures at night. It is a great way to beat the boat traffic and the heat."

Having no luck trolling at Battery Island in spite of switching lure colors and styles several times, we headed farther west to Striking Island, where a creek channel split the island. Oyster beds and sandbars surrounded the boat as I eased the anchor into the water to avoid spooking any trout lurking nearby. Casting grubs to the visible structure, we started catching specks. Once we hit the right color combination, which was yellow jig head with a smoke/metal-flake grub with the tail dipped in chartreuse garlic scent, we switched all our lures to that color combination. We cast upcurrent, letting the lures fall as they came perpendicular to the boat, varying the retrieve until the preferred speed was found.

"Sometimes switching to another area of the river like this is what it takes. When there has been a lot of rain, it influences the

Speckled trout hot spots—Bald Head Island

Courtesy of Maptech

salinity and clarity of the water. The fish tend also to go out to the ocean with the falling tide and return with the rising tide. You just have to keep moving with the tide until you find them."

The fickle fish eventually quit biting, in spite of the offering of several more lure colors. So, we headed to the ADM dock. At this point I was thinking how speckled trout fishing was similar to the run-and-gun tactics of tournament-style largemouth bass fishing.

Anchoring downstream of the dock, we cast grubs without catching trout, but managed to hook some small croakers. Price was happier with the croakers than he would have been if we had caught trout.

"Trout love live baits like mullets, pinfish and menhaden. But these little croakers are the best. There is something about the croaking sound they make that drives big trout wild," said Price.

We headed across the Cape Fear River to Cape Creek north of Bald Head Island and anchored in a hole that had a water depth of twelve feet. Price hooked a croaker through the lips with a wide bend style #42 Eagle Claw hook rigged on a Carolina rig with a swivel and a one-half ounce egg sinker.

"When the sun gets up and it gets hot, the fish move to deeper holes. The best way to catch them is by dropping live baits in the deep holes in creek channels like this one," said Price.

He cast the croaker against the undercut bank. As it sank, it bounced along the bottom, then suddenly stopped. Price let the fish run a rod length, then set the hook with a light snap of the wrist.

"You don't want to set the hook hard or it will tear the trout's mouth," he said. Playing the fish delicately on two pounds of drag tension, he deftly netted the citation-sized speck, then released it. Any other angler would have been whooping and jumping around the boat at this type of success. But Price just smiled as he let the fish go because he routinely catches such bragging-sized specks.

"A trout has a soft mouth, so I use light tackle. I use 6-pound test Silver Thread monofilament, a 6-foot Star medium light graphite spinning rod, and a Shimano Stradic 2000 reel that holds 170 yards of line. The reel has a fast six-to-one retrieve ratio, which helps when the fish are hot in the summer. They swim faster in warm water and it helps keep the line tight because of the light drag tensions you have to use," said Price.

Price says he has no secret holes and that other anglers ply the same waters where he fishes.

"I figure I will always catch my share," he said. "Everyone should get out on the water and enjoy a day of fishing. Having some success always makes it fun."

Ned Connelly unhooks a 75-pound black drum caught from the Cape Fear River.

Carol Marsh catches tiny "sand fleas" from the surf to use for catching Goliath black drum.

Chapter 16

The Beat of a Different Drum

Charles Dycus lives to fish. He works hard at his chosen profession of taxidermy just so he can make enough cash to pay the expenses for trips to the North Carolina coast from his home in Sanford.

Specializing in red drum and sheepshead fishing, he has also developed a penchant for catching huge black drum in recent years.

"We used to fish mostly under the Highway 70 Causeway in Morehead City and on the oyster bars in the Elizabeth River," said Dycus. "But after I heard about the size of the fish they were catching in the lower Cape Fear River, we switched fishing spots. The black drum in Morehead City are nice-sized, up to fifteen pounds or so, with smaller fish in the Elizabeth River."

In the Cape Fear River in August of 1997, Dycus' 10-year-old son, Justin, caught a black drum that weighed fifty pounds. In

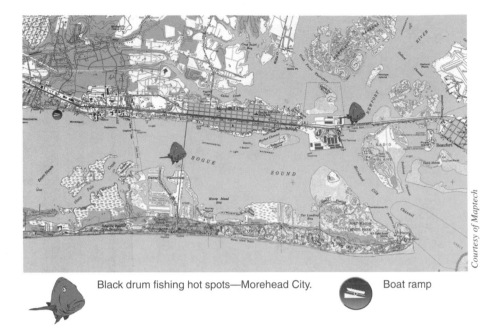

Black drum fishing hot spots—Morehead City.   Boat ramp

Courtesy of Maptech

August of 1998, his wife, Amy, caught one that weighed sixty-two pounds. But the fish he caught a week later on August 11 beat them all. It weighed 100.1 pounds, had a length of fifty-six inches, a girth of forty-six inches and beat the previous North Carolina state record fish by more than thirteen pounds!

Dycus plans to perform a natural skin-mount of his record fish, a difficult project to anyone familiar with the taxidermist's art. But he's skilled enough for the challenge.

The giant black drum was caught on 50-pound test monofilament, matched to a Shimano TR 200 G level-wind reel and a six-foot extra-heavy action rod. Suitable for offshore grouper fishing, this rig is relatively light tackle considering the areas where Dycus fishes.

"I tie up to the bridge pilings at the Morehead City Causeway, and under the ADM dock above Southport in the Cape Fear. Black drum are always caught around heavy structure. The record fish scrubbed the line against the mooring piles under the ADM dock, fraying it for twenty feet above the leader. The piles are covered with oysters and barnacles. It is a wonder the line held at all."

The fight took ten minutes, according to Dycus. He offered the rod to one of his fishing partners, North Carolina Wildlife Enforcement Officer Brian Scruggs. However, Scruggs refused the rod.

Instead, Scruggs and Richard Galloway, the third crewman, helped get the behemoth's head into a cavernous landing net after a seesaw battle. During the battle, Dycus fought the fish on his knees at times due to the overhead walkway of the dock interfering with the rod tip as well as to counteract the strength of the fish. Dycus wisely used the biggest net he could find to land the fish. Gaffs are useless against the poker-chip scales of a black drum.

Dycus' terminal tackle for black drum consists of a Carolina style, sliding sinker rig with a three-ounce egg sinker, a large barrel swivel, a leader of 60-pound wire or 100-pound monofilament and a 5/0 hook. Most anglers would expect a vicious strike from such a huge fish, but it takes a sense of "feel" to detect the nibbling of a monster black drum.

"Fishing for sheepshead is good practice for catching black drum. The bite is like the vibration set up by plucking a guitar string," Dycus said. "Since I fish a lot for sheepshead, I'm used to setting the hook when I feel the slightest sensation of grinding or extra weight on the line."

For bait, Dycus used a tiny sand flea or mole crab — those critters that scramble to and fro, burying themselves along the edge of the breakers where the sea meets the shore on oceanfront beaches. It is hard to believe, but that huge fish was caught on a bait the size of the first joint of Dycus' little finger.

Chumming is part of the equation that equals big fish. Dycus was using "old" sand fleas for chum. Tied beneath the boat in a potato sack to leave a scent trail drifting in the strong current beneath the dock, the chum attracts fish to the area where the hooks are lowered to the bottom. Clams, oysters, crabs or most any other shellfish will also attract black drum when used as bait or chum, but it is uncommon for large black drum to be caught on fin fish of any description, although juvenile fish will take cut mullet and relish

117

fresh shrimp.

The immature fish are easily identified by vertical black stripes on the body, which are similar to those of a sheepshead, rather than the overall dusky appearance of the adults. Once out of the water, the color of adult fish changes from a dark or reddish brown to a charcoal cast.

Another avid angler who fishes for black drum is Ned Connelly of Wilmington. His biggest fish so far weighed a tackle-bashing seventy-five pounds. Whereas Dycus launches his 18-foot skiff from the North Carolina Wildlife Commission's access area in Southport, Connelly travels south from Snow's Cut in a 17-foot center-console.

"It's big water down there, near the Cape Fear River mouth. I have had more than my share of bumpy rides, especially at night. I wouldn't make the trip in a smaller boat except under ideal conditions, although I have seen a lot of johnboats at the old Quarantine Station and at the ADM dock that make the shorter ride up the river from Southport," said Connelly

"My favorite time to fish for big black drum in the heat of the summer is at sunset. I stay out all night and return upriver when the sun comes up. Any wind usually dies down at dawn so the river is calmer. Also, the run up the river can be dangerous in the dark. Crab pots and driftwood are always in the river, and it is easy to find yourself on a sand bar if you don't pay attention to navigation markers.

"The worst conditions occur when the tide is falling and there is a southwest wind blowing against it. It has the same effect as rubbing a cat the wrong way. Those river waves can get mighty angry."

There are several things that Connelly's big fish and the Dycus monster have in common. They were caught two years apart in the month of August. Both were caught on a sand flea during a full moon just after the tide started down from its peak. Both were caught in the middle of the day at the ADM dock and were the only fish boated on the trip.

Both Dycus and Connelly agree that those conditions combine for the best shot at another record fish.

Courtesy o˚Maptech

 Black drum fishing hot spot—Lower Cape Fear River.

"If I were going to make one trip for black drum, it would be during those conditions," said Connelly. "But you never know when they're going to bite. I've seen them caught as early as March and as late as October. But the heat of the summer — June, July and August — seems to be the best time to catch the biggest black drum."

Besides sand fleas, Connelly uses fiddler crabs, rock crabs and blue crabs for bait. He also uses shrimp when other baits are scarce, hooking them through the tail to prevent them from spinning in the current. However, shrimp attract numerous bait-stealers like croak-

119

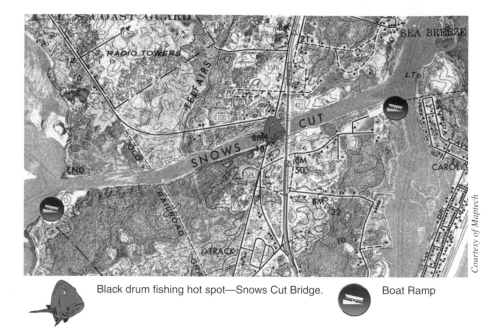

Courtesy of Maptech

Black drum fishing hot spot—Snows Cut Bridge.　　Boat Ramp

ers as well. Sand fleas and rock crabs are skewered in multiples of as many as the hook will hold. Blue crabs are cut in half, the claws and legs removed, and hooked through the shell near the spike. If the legs are left intact, the hook-set can be missed when only a leg is in the fish's mouth. All of these baits can be gathered and frozen for future use.

"The 75-pounder was caught using a sand flea that had been frozen for a year," said Connelly. "It's tough to go to the beach to catch sand fleas and fish the same day. It can take a quart of sand fleas per angler for a day of fishing. Taking the kids to the surf to gather a bunch of sand fleas or to the waterway for a day of crabbing and clamming is a lot of fun. We also catch the silver dollar sized rock crabs by overturning erosion control stones along seawalls. Freezing any of these baits ahead of time makes the actual day of fishing easier."

Many anglers believe black drum to be inferior table fare. But Connelly disagrees.

"As long as they still have stripes, at up to fifteen pounds or so, the meat is very white and firm. It is suitable for any grouper or other white fish recipe. I like to fry the fillets after cutting them into chunks. For the medium fish of up to forty pounds, the fillets can be blackened, Cajun-style, like redfish, or boiled in a fish stew. Once they get over forty pounds, their meat gets rubbery. Unless I'm trying for a record, I like to release the really large fish. Besides the meat being tough, there is about a ten percent chance that the big ones will have too many parasites in their meat to be edible."

For catching black drum, there are lots of other places in the Carolina Beach region to try, according to Connelly.

"The U.S. 421 bridge in Snow's Cut near Carolina Beach is a good spot for smaller fish," said Connelly. "There are some big black drum hooked there, too, but most folks use tackle that is too light to handle the bruisers because they hook them while trying for sheepshead against the wooden abutments. Another good place is the surf at Masonboro Island, especially in the spring and fall. The rocks below Fort Fisher hold lots of small black drum. I heard of one caught along one of the Fort Fisher rock jetties, locally called "The Cribbing," in May of 1998 that weighed sixty-eight pounds. Boat docks along the Inland waterway near Wrightsville Beach also hold small black drum virtually year round. The best docks have pilings that are encrusted with oysters and barnacles. By scraping the barnacles off with a boat paddle during low tide, the angler chums fish to the area when the tide rises to cover the damaged shells. Most anglers don't realize the fish are there because they use fish for bait, or lures that imitate fish, when casting with spinning tackle for red drum around the docks. If they used crabs or sand fleas for bait, they could catch a different drum."

While Dycus' fish was huge, the world record black drum was bigger. It was caught by an angler in Delaware Bay and weighed 113 pounds. It is apparent that there are bigger fish waiting to be caught. While a red drum of fifty pounds is remarkable, a black drum that size is ho-hum. It is no wonder so many anglers who like to catch big fish inshore are listening to the beat of a different drum.

The author caught this seven-pound flounder on a jig with a Powerbait strip.

Chapter 17

Catching Flounder on Artificial Lures

It was a scorching dawn in early September, with heat so unmerciful that the dripping cast net draped over my shoulder only added to the misery created by the coastal lowland humidity. Instead of evaporating, the saltwater droplets running off the net merely added to the sweat that had already glued my shirt to my chest and shoulders.

Other anglers were wearing themselves out in the heat as well, throwing nets near Carolina Beach Inlet that came up with one or two mullet per cast. It was hardly an enjoyable experience. But it was a necessary chore, or so I thought at the time. "First catch bait, then go fishing," was once the only tried and true recipe for catching flounder.

Eventually, I snagged the cast net on an oyster bed. Attempts to free it ripped a gaping hole in the mesh and cut several lead lines. The net was rendered useless. All floundered out for the day, I headed for the Wrightsville Beach jetties to cast a bucktail jig in an attempt to seduce a few red drum.

As I stair-stepped the jig downward to the bottom of the rocks, it met resistance when it should have landed on the sandy floor of Masonboro Inlet. Setting the hook, I fought the fish to the boat. Instead of a red drum, however, I netted a nice flounder. Thinking that catching a flounder on a jig was accidental, I cast again to the same spot. *Surprise!* I hooked another flounder. Another cast met the same result, then another, until I had eight fine flatfish flopping in the ice chest within just a few minutes. However, the lesson didn't strike home at the time, and I bought another cast net the next day to rejoin the anglers wasting precious fishing time trying to catch live bait and working hard to keep their live well pumps, batteries and switches functioning.

In the twenty years since, I certainly have caught my share of

Using lures to catch flounder saves the fishing time lost while catching live baits.

flounder on artificial lures. However, as on that long-ago lucky day, those flounder have mostly been caught by accident when pursuing other species. That is until three years ago, when a famous saltwater fishing guide changed the way I will catch flounder forevermore, when he mentioned a jig and plastic trailer combination he used for catching flatfish.

Jimmy Price owns a tackle shop in Southport, N.C. and operates *Wreck Hunter Guide Fishing Service* as well. Price showed me his special flounder-jigging combination. It consisted of a high-quality jig with hard epoxy paint laid on in multiple coats. Impaled on the jig's stainless steel hook was a plastic tail designed specifically for enticing flounder, having a split tail, pearl white color, and being impregnated with a flounder-attracting scent when it was cast in the mold.

"It all started several years back," said Price. "I have been using artificial lures for catching flounder for over fifteen years now, whereas I used to drift with cut bait or use live bait like most other anglers."

Price is quick to point out that he did not accidentally happen upon the idea, but became obsessed with the technique after seeing a video about using artificial lures for catching flatfish. Price has always been a competitive fisherman, and recently won the U.S. Anglers' Association 1999 Angler of the Year Award for catching the largest aggregate weight of several species in the state, including flounder.

"I wanted to be as good or better than anyone else at catching flounder. So, if artificial lures would do the trick, I wanted to try them. I got as many different types of lures as I could and really enjoyed using them. I started out with bucktails and used a minnow or cut bait as a trailer. I loved the way you could feel the strike. It isn't like waiting to set the hook when using a minnow and not knowing for sure the fish is still there. With an artificial lure, you set the hook the instant you feel the bump that indicates a flounder has inhaled the lure."

Eventually, however, Price decided that if a jig and minnow combination would work well for flounder, so would a jig with a soft-plastic trailer. While most anglers were still drifting minnows on bottom rigs behind a boat moving with the current, Price began anchoring his boat and casting lures into the "junk yards" of boat docks, fish houses, and marinas around the mouth of the Cape Fear River.

"The secret in using a jig is anchoring up and fishing around piers, bulkheads, poles, oyster beds, wrecks and rock piles," said Price. "I cast upcurrent and then I hop the lure back to me. You have to make the lure seem alive like a shrimp, wounded minnow or squid. I jerk it up about six to eight inches above the bottom and never more than one foot. By making it look like a baitfish that is wounded and fluttering to the bottom just before it dies, a flounder will think he has found easy prey and will instinctively strike it."

Price prefers plastic trailers that are patterned after squid. He once used shark belly skins, which he split like a bass angler's pork-rind bait, as well as squid strips, to add a fluttering action. However, Price said he quit using shark belly skins once the plastic Berkley

Power Bait Flounder Strips came along.

The bucktails he prefers to use weigh 5/8-ounce and have stainless steel hooks, such as the jigs manufactured by Hank Brown. Such top quality bucktails are expensive. However, where Price fishes, the lures can take a lot of abuse. He said that cheaply made bucktails have the paint beaten off within a few casts when fishing some of the areas with the hardest structure like the Archer-Daniels-Midland dock in the lower Cape Fear River or along the rocky bottom structure on either side of the Southport municipal fishing pier. Price also likes to fish near Poor Charlie's Fish House in Southport, an area that is loaded with shell-encrusted pilings. He says when fishing around Poor Charlie's Fish House, it is important to watch for commercial vessels coming to unload their catch and stay out of the way.

"When you want to catch big flounder, you have to be willing to pay the price," said Price. "The really big fish are structure oriented. You must be willing to lose tackle in order to be successful. You don't want to use a poorly made jig that will have the paint chipped off after a few casts. It's the same as losing a lure that is hung on structure. A damaged lure must be replaced, so the lure is lost. It pays an angler to select quality bucktails and jig heads.

"Plastic trailers are just so much easier to use than natural baits, especially squid. Squid is very messy and smelly and the bait-stealers like pinfish jump on it so bad. The plastic flounder strips are tough and durable, which helps them catch more fish because you don't have to change bait or add bait after it has been struck by a non-target fish."

Lures are also more challenging and sporting according to Price. Price says he can "really cook" in a competition against a live bait fishermen by out-catching him at least three flounder to one. But the key to his success is also found in a simple flip of the wrist.

"When you are hopping the bait, you snap your wrist up from about about ten o'clock to twelve o'clock in quick jerks while taking in one or two reel turns. A flounder usually hits the lure on the fall. You have to set the hook the instant you feel the bump of a strike."

Price uses a seven-foot, bait-casting rod and reel combination loaded with low-stretch monofilament line. He claims that super lines don't work as well because there has to be some give when he sets the hook or the hook can be jerked out of the flounder's jaw. Also, spotted sea trout are present in waters frequented by flatfish. Sea trout have notoriously tender mouths. No-stretch lines will jerk free of a sea trout's mouth under the power used to set the hook upon a flounder strike.

"I want a rod that is of medium weight with a stiff tip and some backbone," said Price. "When you set the hook, you have to lift the fish free of the bottom and start him toward you. That will keep him away from snags. I use 8-pound test and set the drag at two to three pounds of tension."

Unless non-believers doubt that big flounder can be landed with artificial lures on such flimsy tackle, Price points out that his biggest flounder weighed seventeen pounds, six ounces, and was caught on an artificial lure fished on six-pound test monofilament line.

Brandon Keith caught this red drum at Wrightsville Beach using fly tackle.

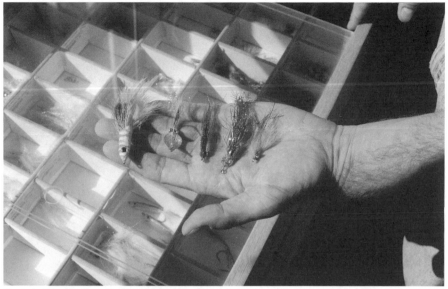

Captain Tyler Stone's favorite flies for catching red drum while poling a boat in shallow water. From left to right are shown: Joe's Mullet, Spoonfly, Clouser Minnow in sculpin pattern, Copperhead Fly, Clouser Minnow in bonefish pattern.

Chapter 18

Copper-Headed Fish on a Copperhead Fly

Captain Tyler Stone gently eased his boat across a submerged oyster bed, its hull barely clearing serrated razor shell-edges that could scrape the bottom at any moment and spook his intended quarry. His push pole made no splash as he positioned the boat for a cast from his client who was standing as still as a statue on the bow.

"Ten o'clock, forty feet," Stone whispered.

Matt Martin delicately flipped a fly in the direction indicated by Stone. Sunlight gleamed off the gaudy fly like Christmas lights twinkling off tinsel as it arced through the air. In an instant, its fire was extinguished as it submerged beneath the mirrored surface of gin-clear saltwater.

Courtesy of Maptech

 Red drum fishing hot spots—Topsail.   Boat Ramp

"Too far! Strip, strip, strip! Set the hook!" hissed Stone.

Although Martin could not see the fish strike the fly, Stone had a grandstand seat for the event. Elevated by a poling platform, Stone saw every move the fish made in the millimeters-deep water.

After the hook-set, Martin used his thumb and forefinger to create friction against the fly line, methodically slowing the rhythmic moves of the red drum. In the length of a waltz, the dance was over. The tired fish rested beside the gunwale. As she caught her breath, she rolled on her side. The midday sunlight glinted metallically from the coppery scales of her head and the hackles of the fly kissing her lip.

Without taking the fish from the water Stone released her from the fly's grip. Recovering quickly, she swam away to rejoin a school of fifty of her kin. Stone eased the boat along to find another dancing partner for the Copperhead Fly.

Stone is a fishing guide and owns *Intracoastal Angler* tackle shop at Wrightsville Beach, which caters only to fly-fishermen. Having cast flies along the best fishing waters of the United States, it seems curious that he would select the southeastern coast of North Carolina as his watery backyard. However, his talent and techniques have created a sensation new to this locality that also allowed him to achieve a life-long goal.

"I used to fly-fish for Spanish mackerel, false albacore and bonito," said Stone. "However, I am approaching the point where I will be targeting red drum exclusively, because that is what everybody really wants to catch."

Stone has fished flats in Florida and South Carolina. Catching red drum while poling shallow craft in those states is a common practice. He believed that the same type of fishing could be done successfully in North Carolina. Two events came together to help Stone achieve his goal of guiding clients to consistent action.

"The return of red drum is a Mid-Atlantic and Gulf of Mexico phenomenon," said Stone. "The fish are back after having been over-fished for years. The net bans in Florida and Gulf States have helped, while in the Carolinas harvest restrictions are having a positive effect. The numbers of fish we are seeing did not exist a few years ago."

The other event is the increasing popularity of fly-fishing. Stone said that interest in his tackle shop and guide service has grown exponentially the last four years, because many people that move to the area have knowledge of that type of equipment and local anglers seeking new thrills are catching the excitement.

"People really want to hunt these fish, once they hear about them," said Stone. "Poling the boat through a marsh looking for fish and casting to them is more hunting than fishing. Seeing a school, casting to it, then fighting and releasing a single fish is enough excitement for anyone. This is not the type of fishing where you load the boat with fish, but the thrill level is high."

To navigate shallows, Stone added an 8-foot platform to his Hewes flats boat. The platform raises his eyes to eleven feet above the water.

"My job is to see the fish and move the boat in areas that are impossible to reach using a motor," said Stone. "I can see sixty feet while the client scans the water near the boat. There's lots of team-work involved."

Stone sets the boat up with the tide and the wind to his back to make maneuvering easy. However, he said it is more important that the sun is at his back so he can see fish.

"I always enter a creek with eliminating the sun's glare as my primary concern," said Stone.

Stone finds red drum in the marshes of Masonboro Island, Figure Eight Island, Bald Head Island, and Elmore's Inlet. The key is spending lots of time looking in these areas on different tides.

"Finding areas that hold fish on low tide is important," said Stone. "Poling into a marsh on high tide and fishing falling tide will sometimes trap a boat in a pocket of water. Letting the tide catch you can be one of the most productive ways to fish. All of the fish will be concentrated in a deep hole at low tide."

Stone said that anglers must be conservative when fishing a school. Like a quail hunter maintaining a favorite covey by shoot-

Red drum fishing hot spots—Pages Creek.

ing only a bird or two, a fly-fishermen should catch and release only a couple of fish from each school.

"You can't pound a school," said Stone. "You can't pressure them day after day, or they will move. You should catch a couple of fish, then hunt for another school. A good day for sight-casting to redfish will produce as many as twenty releases. But one quality fish can be a good day if you get to see lots of fish."

To enable him to spot fish below the surface, Stone wears amber-tinted, polarized glasses. The amber lens provides contrast while cutting glare.

Courtesy of Maptech

Red drum fishing hot spots—Wrightsville Beach.　　Boat Ramp

Since the fish are usually invisible to the angler because of his low vantage point, Stone practices directing the angler's casts before entering the fishing area. With the angler on the bow of the boat, he calls the 12 o'clock position straight ahead, 3 o'clock to starboard and 9 o'clock to port. Other positions are referred to like the numbers on a clock. Distances are judged based on his estimates and observance of the angler's casting skill.

Stone uses a fast-action, 8-weight rod manufactured by Sage or Scott with matching reel and floating line. The single-action reel has a capacity of 200 yards of backing. The backing is usually insignificant due to the shortness of most casts and battles. However, an occasional bull redfish can strip line down into the backing. Leaders are 12- to 20-pound monofilament.

"I like to catch six- to ten-pound fish by using the reel and use finger pressure only against the line for fighting smaller fish," said

Stone. "If you horse a big drum, the leader can break. I prefer to let the drag wear down the large fish."

His favorite flies are the Copperhead and Spoonfly, tied by Randy Martin out of South Carolina, as well as a Clouser minnow tied in sculpin or bonefish pattern, and a Joe's Mullet.

"The Copperhead just has so much flash that the fish can't resist," said Stone. "The Copperhead and Clousers ride point-up to prevent snags. Also, the Spoonfly rides point-up. These flies can be cast ahead of a fish and allowed to fall to the bottom. As the fish approaches, the angler strips line, making them look like shrimp jumping. Joe's Mullet is a floating fly."

Another Wrightsville Beach Guide is Bill Douglass. Douglass discovered fly-fishing for redfish by a different route than Stone.

"I began as a bait fishermen," said Douglass. "The bait always started to show up in April when the water warmed and I was chartering Spanish and bonito. However, on windy days, I fished inside."

That was in the limitless days of red drum fishing when a full cooler was important. However, with regulation came a consciousness about the resource that soon led to the use of artificial lures on windy, redfish days. Live baits caused loss of some fish due to the fish swallowing the hook. Artificial lures became the answer.

Fly-fishing and conservation go together, according to Douglass. With the limit on red drum at one fish in 2000, there is not much demand for keeping fish.

"Less experienced anglers had good luck with live bait," said Douglass. "But soon the skill level of my clients increased and they preferred artificial lures because of the direct connection to the fish during the strike. I found that I have to keep one step ahead of clients to keep them excited. By showing them how to fly fish, I teach them something new. I had always fished channels and docks with clients and began fly-fishing on my own. What I found out was that the catch level is just as high, because you don't waste your time on water that doesn't hold fish."

Douglass fishes in a 20-foot Sea Mark boat, manufactured in

Rocky Point, North Carolina. The center-console design has a V-bow, but also has a flat bottom. The design is stable offshore and is easy to pole in one foot of water from atop its platform.

Even with the shallow-draft boat, Douglass wears boots, because he often gets out and wades. He once poled up a creek, but had to wade when the water depth decreased to six inches. He found over one hundred puppy drum and caught a few before having to pole out ahead of a falling tide.

Unlike Stone, Douglass likes to fish the last two hours of the rising tide through the first two hours of the falling tide. Many flats he fishes are completely dry at low tide.

"An astronomical tide is especially good," said Douglass. "The flood tide lets fish feed in areas they can't normally reach and they just go wild. You can see them working in the grass. When the tide falls, you cast to the edges of grass beds and have good luck. Also, the higher tides let you fish another hour on rise and fall."

At low tide, Douglass concentrates on feeder creeks that have as little as eighteen inches of water. He fishes the same areas as Stone and uses the same general types of tackle, except he prefers Loomis rods and has different tastes in flies. He also adds Pages Creek to his list of fishing areas.

"Pages Creek is deep enough to allow fly-fishing from any boat that can be poled," said Douglass. "The water is clear and lets you see well."

"I like the Copperhead fly in muddy water," said Douglass. "But orange and red Clousers are also hot. The muddier the water, the brighter the fly, is my rule for red drum. I also like a Cave's Wobbler, a small gold spoon. You cast it and let it sit on the bottom until the fish approaches, then twitch it up."

Stone and Douglass agree on one point emphatically — sportsmanship. They feel that anyone who approaches a boat being poled is inviting hot tempers.

Approaching a sight-fishing party spooks their fish. In shallow areas where sight-fishing is practiced, there is no excuse for getting too close. Out on the flats, there is plenty of elbowroom for everyone. The best idea if someone beats you to an area is finding another spot to hunt for fish.

Red drum fishing hot spots—Wrightsville Beach. Boat Ramp

Courtesy of Maptech

137

The author caught this weakfish by jigging a spoon on a rock ledge one mile offshore of Masonboro Island.

A net is mandatory for landing weakfish due to their fragile mouths. Since weakfish can be picky, it pays to select jigging spoons in a wide variety of colors.

Chapter 19

Cash in on the Strong Return of Weakfish

It was one of those balmy December days that duck hunters curse. There was no wind at all and the air temperature was soaring into the 70's. I was stacking up decoys after an over-heated and foolhardy attempt at shooting a few ducks on the Cape Fear River when Ned Connelly turned into my driveway.

"It's too hot for hunting ducks," said Connelly. "Do you want to try catching some gray trout?"

Gray trout, also called weakfish because of the paper-thin membranes of their delicate mouths, are one of the tastiest fish on the Carolina Coast. Connelly knew that I had caught a nice bunch of them the previous weekend and wanted to cash in on what I had found.

It didn't take much arm-twisting for Connelly to convince me to give up on the waterfowl. He helped me remove the decoys and

Buddy Connelly with a limit of weakfish caught near Kure Beach.

shotgun from my boat and we replaced them with tackle boxes and medium-weight spinning rods.

The water was so slick during the trip out of the usually rollicking Carolina Beach Inlet that water didn't even splash over the sides of my 19-foot duck boat. The ocean was as flat as a pane of ice-blue glass. In less than one hour after Connelly turned into the driveway, we were anchoring at the Phillip Wolfe Reef located a couple of miles off Kure Beach.

"I heard from Steve Lebanac at *Seagull Bait and Tackle* at Carolina Beach that anglers were catching gray trout on these spoons. The beauty of the Gibbs jigging spoon is that it can be bent to give greater or lesser action to find the type of action the trout prefer on a particular day," I told Connelly as he tied the gold Gibbs

Minnow I handed him onto his line.

I selected a blue-and-white spoon from a paper sack. There were several other colors in the sack as well. Before I could tie the lure to my line, Connelly was hooked up to his first fish. Setting down my rod, I netted a hard-fighting gray trout for Connelly that weighed nearly three pounds.

While Connelly unhooked his fish, I finished tying on a lure and free-spooled it to the bottom by opening the bail of my spinning reel. Tripping the bail when the slack in the line indicated the lure had run out of water, I twitched the lure upward and retrieved a couple of turns of the reel handle as Connelly had done. The lure reached the top of its arc and I allowed it to sink. The spoon was struck by a gray trout the twin of Connelly's before it hit bottom again.

We had one less than a limit of gray trout apiece in one-half hour of fishing, but continued catch-and-release fishing in an attempt to catch a citation-sized fish of six pounds. As we fished, boats began to arrive all around us after making the 2 1/2-mile trip from Carolina Beach Inlet. Before long there were two-dozen boats anchored nearby. Most of the anglers began catching fish but few experienced the luck we were having. Many anglers were spending more time trying to free lures and rigs from the bottom structure than fighting fish.

"It is amazing to me that out of all this structure, there are only a couple of hot spots where the gray trout really stack up," I told Connelly. "I watched a boat anchor over this spot last week and line up the AR 378 buoy with one of the condominium projects on the

Courtesy of Maptech

Weakfish fishing hot spot—AR378.

Courtesy of Maptech

Weakfish fishing hot spot—AR420 and AR 425.

beach. If you aren't fishing in just the right spot like the captain of that boat, you will probably still catch a limit, but it will take more work. Jigging an ounce-and-a-half spoon up and down all day in forty feet of water can get tiring to the wrists."

Artificial Reef 378 consists of a jumbled pile of tires bound together and sunk that has deteriorated over the span of thirty years. There are also three barges that were sunk in the area. The barges and tires are covered with marine growth, which makes a generous supply of jigging spoons a necessity when going after gray trout. After breaking several spoons off on the structure, we decided to give up our honey hole to other anglers as the crowd began casting right under our boat.

"Let's head on up to the Myrtle Bushes and fish the hard bottom at John's Creek to see what's there," I said to Connelly. "Steve Lebanac told me they were really catching gray trout up there last week."

When we finished the seven-mile trip north toward Masonboro Inlet, we found about three dozen boats drifting or anchored over an area of about one-half square mile. Connelly reviewed the evidence and noted, "This must be the spot."

Nobody seemed to be catching fish. The water was calm enough that we could see a lack of angler activity in all directions.

"The best way to fish a big area like John's Creek is by drifting along on the prevailing current or wind," I told Connelly. "By jigging spoons while the boat is moving, you can explore a lot of territory until you find a concentration of fish. The bottom in this area is rocky and you need to make sure to bounce the lure and that you do not allow the lure to drag along the bottom or you will get it hung on a rock."

However, in spite of making several wind-propelled drifts and jigging over hundreds of yards of rocky bottom, the only gray trout we could catch were as small as the fish we had already caught.

. Luckily, we did have success with Virginia mullet. They would play "tag" with the jigging spoons and gaff themselves in the gill plates instead of their mouths. They weren't gray trout, but we had enough grays for dinner, so we fished with two-hook bottom rigs baited with shrimp and added some nice Virginia mullets to the gray trout in the ice chest.

Another angler who has great success with gray trout is Doug Cutting, who operates *Fishhawk Guide Service* out of Southport. I spoke with Cutting to pry loose some of his secrets for catching gray trout.

"Gray trout have really been on the upswing for the last two years," said Cutting. "The best fishing for grays runs from October through mid-December. However, I have caught them off the Carolina Beach Tire Reef as late as June."

Cutting likes to use medium spinning gear and 10-pound-test monofilament line for catching gray trout. The lightness of the rod keeps fatigue to a minimum for his clients as well as providing a good fight from the fish. He also feels that light tackle helps to prevent the hook from ripping out of the mouth of the fish.

"Gray trout are really strong fighters," said Cutting. "I had one day in December when all the fish we caught weighed between six and seven pounds. That size of fish will put a good bend in a light rod in thirty feet of water. But you can't put too much pressure on them or the hooks will pull loose. They have a soft mouth and that is why gray trout are also called weakfish."

Cutting prefers to catch gray trout at the Tom McGlammery Reef (AR 420) and at the Yaupon Beach Reef (AR 425) after heading out of the Cape Fear River mouth at Southport. He also said that he catches lots of gray trout while casting MirrOlures and jigs with plastic grub tails for speckled trout in the creeks and off structure near the river mouth.

"I fish the McGlammery Reef more than the Yaupon Reef," said Cutting. "Usually, I drift across the reef while casting Sting Silver spoons. I like chartreuse-and-white or silver spoons. Once I find the fish by jigging with a spoon, I anchor up and fish with small, live menhaden. Gray trout will eat just about anything. They really like live shrimp, but can be caught on dead shrimp as well."

When fishing Yaupon Reef, Cutting typically begins jigging within twenty yards of the buoy. As the boat drifts, he uses a depth finder to search for the structure. He also watches other fishermen to see where the fish are concentrated.

"Once you start fishing, you don't want the spoon to drag along the bottom or it will get hung up," said Cutting. "You want the lure to barely bounce the bottom, then lift it while taking in one crank of the reel handle. If you keep the slack out of the line, the strike is easy to detect.

"The best conditions for catching gray trout are clean, cool water and a calm day. Generally speaking, I find that the cleaner the water, the better the bite."

A weakfish to a commercial fisherman is called a gray trout by a sport angler. The fish was a very valuable commercial resource in North Carolina until populations crashed. In the late 1980's the catch was equally divided among recreational anglers and commercial fishermen. By 1993 however, the recreational take was just fifteen percent of the total catch and reached a low point with a landing of 70,000 pounds.

Average recreational landings were 125,454 pounds, statistically, between 1988 and 1998. However, by 1998 the recreational catch had climbed to 185,588 pounds. The NCDMF stock status for weakfish was listed as "recovering" in 1999.

According to Dr. Louis Daniel, Executive Assistant to Councils, "The outlook is strong for weakfish. Anglers did so well they began asking for an increase in bag limits and size limits. The recovering population of the fish allowed a size limit increase from twelve to fourteen inches and bag limit increase from four to ten fish in 1999."

The big factor in restoring the fish has been the reduction in the commercial catch. A management plan underwent several amendments between 1985 and 1996. The plan increased mesh sizes in trawls and seines to allow juvenile weakfish to escape. Fly nets, which are huge ocean trawls that open to as large as 100 feet by 150 feet, were banned south of Cape Hatteras due to their devastating effects on weakfish that were only a few inches long and were caught primarily as by-catch to other targeted fish like herring. Fly nets can catch 40,000 pounds of fish in a single, 45-minute tow.

"Merely by closing the area south of Cape Hatteras to fly nets, North Carolina met its harvest reductions to comply with the weakfish management plan as required by the Atlantic States Coastal Cooperative Management Act," said Daniel. "Additionally, we began requiring fin-fish bypass devices in shrimp trawls that saved ten million weakfish per year. We are also looking at inshore pound nets and long-haul seines to see if their effects on juvenile weakfish can be reduced. Typically, a nine-inch fish is age one and a 12-inch fish is age two. A 14-inch recreational limit ensures two spawns before the fish is removed from the population by an angler, because weakfish mature at nine inches to eleven inches in length."

Carol Marsh caught this nice spotted sea trout on a live mullet fished on float rig.

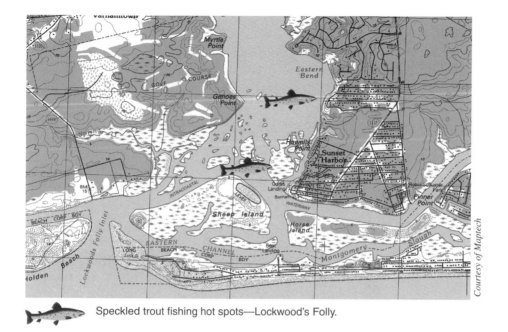

Speckled trout fishing hot spots—Lockwood's Folly.

Chapter 20

Freezer Filling Sea Trout

By December most of the saltwater inshore fishing is winding down. However, those anglers who brave the cold or venture out on those precious Carolina days when temperatures reach the 50's usually set out with the intention of catching speckled trout. There is good speckled trout fishing along the entire coast, if the temperature doesn't get cold enough to freeze the surface of the backwaters.

Many guides along the Carolina Coast specialize in helping their clients catch freezers full of speckled trout. While the location of a trout fishing hotspot is a closely guarded secret among recreational anglers, some of the state's top guides willingly share information

147

about some of their favorite places.

David Mammay who operates *Reel Success Guide Fishing Service* is best known for catching trophy flounder. But when the water chills, he switches to speckled trout in the waters near Southport.

"The Lockwood's Folly River has some of the best speckled trout fishing in this area," said Mammay. "There are oyster beds from the river mouth to upstream at least ten miles. When you run out of oyster beds going upstream, you run out of the trout. There is an oyster bed that runs across the river channel at marker No. 5 that is real productive."

The river is tricky to fish if you aren't familiar with the channels and bars, according to Mammay. But the oyster beds are the key to consistently catching winter specks.

"An angler should study the Lockwood's Folly River at low tide," said Mammay. "The key is locating the oyster beds in the river during low water, then returning to fish the beds when the tide is high. An area must have structure to hold trout."

When fishing an oyster bed, Mammay uses a lead-head jig with a plastic grub tail, a MirrOlure or a live shrimp on a float rig.

"When using an artificial lure, I anchor the boat where I can cast up current and let the lure fall until it touches bottom, then start the retrieve," said Mammay. "I try to retrieve the lure just above the bottom because that's where the trout will be holding. For shrimp, I use a popping cork on my float rigs. By setting the float so the shrimp drifts just off the bottom, it keeps the hook from snagging and keeps the bait at the proper depth. I pop the float as the shrimp drifts across the bed to attract attention to the bait.

"As the tide falls, I anchor where I can cast to the outside of a bend in the channel or a hole in the corner of an oyster bed because the trout will move to these deeper holes on low tide."

Mammay likes to use chartreuse jigs and grub tails. For MirrOlures he says to go with light and bright colors because the water in the Lockwood's Folly is clear.

"The MirrOlures have got to have spots to attract the most

Courtesy of Maptech

 Speckled trout fishing hot spots—Mason Inlet and Rich Inlet.

strikes from speckled trout. For some reason specks like the speckles that make the lure look like a trout, and the lures with spots will out-catch the solid colors two to one."

For fishing water deeper than ten feet, Mammay prefers to troll a secret lure he hasn't yet told anyone about. "One day, no one was catching anything, so I began trolling a Mini Rat-L-Trap. It was gold and looked like a menhaden. I caught sixteen trout that day, so now I fish it all the time. It dives deeper than other lures. By letting line out until the lure ticks the bottom, then reeling in until it is just off the bottom, I catch lots of fish when they're deep."

For landing fish, Mammay uses a rubber net because the hooks will not foul as they will a nylon net. MirrOlures are notorious for snagging a landing net just as the biggest trout of the day slides over the edge of the hoop, letting the fish pull free.

The best access to the Lockwood's Folly is from the North Carolina Wildlife Resources Commission (NCWRC) Boating Access Area at Holden Beach Bridge.

Wrightsville Beach fishing guide Tyler Stone, who operates

149

Intracoastal Angler Guide Service and a fly-fishing shop by the same name, says Mason Inlet and Rich Inlet at the opposite ends of Figure Eight Island are good bets for catching speckled trout.

"Mason Inlet at the south end of Figure Eight Island is a top trout destination," said Stone. "There is a deep channel right against the western bank that holds lots of speckled trout in winter. Lots of fly-fishermen fish the bank all the way up from the inlet to the first creek. The key is fishing the last two hours of the falling tide and the first two hours of the rising tide. During higher tides, the current really rips through the area, so it is difficult to get your fly or lure down to near the bottom where the fish are holding."

Stone says anglers in johnboats and skiffs can easily reach Mason Inlet by launching at the Wrightsville Beach NCWRC ramp. The channel behind Figure Eight Island is shallow, so the best navigation is on high tide. The angler can then fish the falling water and go back out the channel to the Intracoastal Waterway when the high tide returns.

"Rich Inlet at the north end of Figure Eight Island is another good bet for speckled trout," said Stone. "It takes a bigger boat because the best fishing is in the channel on the north side just after you go out through the inlet. When the wind blows, the inlet gets rough. I usually anchor right in the hole, which is 12- to 16-feet deep, and fish the bars on both sides."

Stone prefers a chartreuse Fin-S grub on a red 3/8-ounce Hank Brown jig head, but adjusts the weight of the head depending on water depth and current flow to keep the lure near the bottom. For fly-fishing, he uses a chartreuse/yellow or chartreuse/white Clouser minnow or white Chromashad.

For casting lures, he uses a light-action spinning rod with six-pound-test line. He prefers a line that is very limp, so it casts smoothly, and is very abrasion-resistant. The small diameter of 6-pound-test line allows the lure to fall fast. For fly-fishing, he uses a 7-weight line with a sinking tip.

Stone's advice for catching winter specks is simple.

"When fishing in the cold weather, just remember the fish are

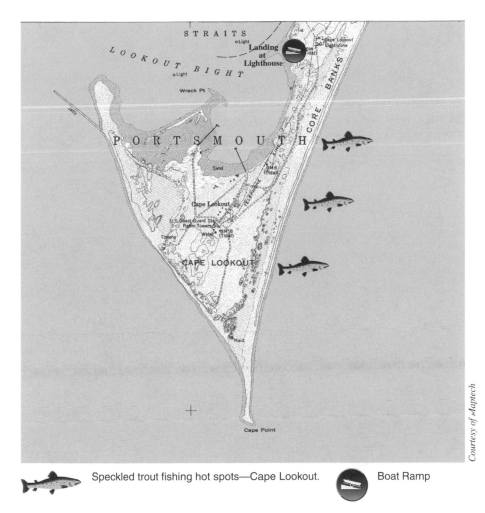

Speckled trout fishing hot spots—Cape Lookout.   Boat Ramp

Courtesy of Maptech

sluggish, so retrieve the lure or fly slowly and be patient," he said. "Keep the lure right on the bottom and you will catch trout."

Rob Pasfield at the *Harker's Island Fishing Center* says catching specks near Morehead City depends upon the weather.

"If the weather is warm, and water temperatures remain above the mid-50s, the North River between Harker's Island and Beaufort holds lots of speckled trout," said Pasfield. "If the water turns cold though, the trout head outside the inlets."

Pasfield targets oyster beds and deep holes when fishing inshore waters. The three-foot tide in the North River can be tricky, so he

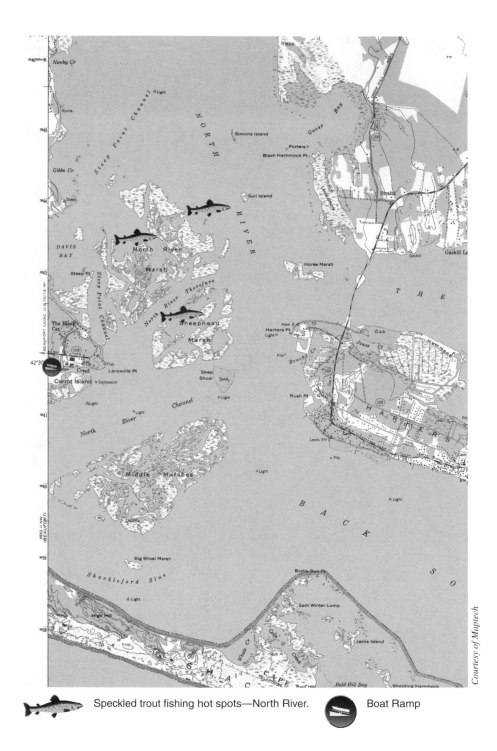

Speckled trout fishing hot spots—North River.   Boat Ramp

152

advises starting a fishing trip on a high tide. Skiffs and johnboats are the best boats for fishing the area due to their shallow draft.

"If you start fishing on the high tide, try the little flats and dips. The water is anywhere from zero to twenty feet deep and averages nine feet to twelve feet in the best holes. I look for a channel right next to an oyster bed and try to anchor within casting range of both."

Pasfield prefers lead-head jigs with plastic grubs to lures because he can fish them right on the bottom where the trout are located. Multiple-hook lures tend to snag on the oyster shells, and are more expensive to replace when lost from the inevitable cutoffs by shells. He uses a red or orange head with a chartreuse or clear/crystal-flake grub body.

Live shrimp or finger-sized mullets are even better than jigs, according to Pasfield. In the deeper holes, he fishes a bottom rig, and uses a float rig to drift live baits above the oyster beds. He also uses floats to fish live baits along the edges of grass beds. Where grass beds are adjacent to an oyster bed that is also near a channel, he feels that a live shrimp suspended beneath a float is the best trout bait of all.

The feeder creeks in the North River Thorofare are good producers of specks. The best time to fish the creek mouths is during a falling tide. That's when baitfish concentrate as they are forced to leave the security of the grass. The mouths of Taylor's Creek and Middle Marsh have oyster beds and channels that hold lots of specks.

If weather turns cold, the speckled trout leave the marshes and rivers and head out into the Atlantic, according to Pasfield. Anglers who still want to catch fish head to Core Banks. On Core Banks, East Beach, Cape Lookout, The Point, and the sloughs by the Cape Lookout Lighthouse are all well-known trout areas.

"The trout vary in size on the Banks," he said. "You can catch anything from keeper size fish right on up to six pounds."

The ferries that run to Core Banks shut down in early December, so anglers must use their own transportation to get to Core Banks. After the nine-mile trip from the launching ramp in Beaufort, anglers can land at the National Park Service dock or at the lighthouse. Some of the best sloughs are within walking distance of the lighthouse.

"The best thing to do is to travel along the beach to find the sloughs on low tide and fish those sloughs on the high tide," said Pasfield. "The sloughs run parallel to the shore with a bar on the outside."

Pasfield said a cloudy or overcast day is best. But it is a good idea to head out to the Banks for trout whenever the wind does not blow hard enough to make the trip hazardous in a small boat.

Favored lures for casting from the beach are MirrOlures and jigs with plastic grub bodies. Long spinning rods with light lines of 6- or 8-pound test are used to create as much distance as possible when casting the relatively light lures.

Epilogue

Inshore Angler was not written with the expectation that its wisdom will be left languishing at home, gathering dust on a bookshelf. Any angler who wants to improve his fishing skills should keep a copy of this book aboard his small boat and carry a copy into his favorite tackle shop as a reference guide when asking questions about lures, rigs, baits and techniques for coastal fishing.

No book about any type of fishing is absolutely complete. There is always a different type of fish to catch, a new technique to try, or a different area to fish. However, once an angler has mastered the techniques for catching the popular species discussed in *Inshore Angler*, he will also have the ability to catch any other fish that makes its home in inshore waters.

To hone his fishing skills, an angler should fish with professional guides, visit his local tackle shops often, and join fishing clubs and conservation organizations. He should also spend every minute possible out on the water. Nothing helps bring about the "fishermen's luck" of being in the right place at the right time more often than simple persistence.

While the expert advice held in these pages is guaranteed to make anyone a better angler, the knowledge earned must be used with the highest regard for the outdoor experience. All size and bag limits for game fish must be strictly followed and any fish that is not destined for immediate use should be returned to the water unharmed. Every animal has a purpose. Even non-target fish commonly regarded as nuisances by anglers have their places in the natural order and must be allowed to complete their cycles of life. It must always be remembered that while catching fish can enhance the enjoyment of a day on the water, it should never become the ultimate goal of time spent outdoors. All anglers should enjoy the glorious colors of sunrises and sunsets, relish the refreshing coolness of sea breezes on sun-reddened cheeks, savor the aroma of salty air and cherish the times spent on the water with friends and family members away from the pressures of day-to-day existence. Trying to catch fish is merely an excuse for taking a relaxing boat ride and reestablishing a bond with Earth. Nothing can make an angler happier—or humbler—than catching a single fish during an entire day of dedicated angling and eating it for supper or releasing it to fight another day.

Until we meet out on the water, I wish all inshore anglers "Tight lines!"

Mike Marsh

Glossary

Glossary

Aft - Rear area of a boat.

* Albright knot - A style of knot used to connect a monofilament line directly to a wire leader.

Alewife (*Alosa pseudoharengus*) - A small, silvery fish with a greenish back that feeds on plankton, travels in schools and can be caught in a cast net and used as bait.

Amidships - The middle of a boat, halfway between the bow and stern.

Anchor - A heavy, metal implement with hooks or flukes to grip the bottom attached by a rope to the boat.

Anchovies (*Anchoa sp.*) - Any of several species of fragile minnows that are caught with cast nets and used as bait.

Anodized aluminum - Aluminum made resistant to corrosion by an electrical process that deposits a coating.

ADM - Archer Daniels Midland Company

Bait-casting reel - See revolving spool reel.

Baitfish - Any small fish used for bait.

Ballyhoo (*Hemiramphus brasiliensis*) - A baitfish widely used in trolling for big game fish. The beak or bill extending from the lower jaw helps in rigging the bait to keep it from spinning at high speeds.

Bass crankbait - A style of lure that dives when retrieved.

Beetle Spin - Trade name for a lure consisting of a jig-and-grub from which protrudes a top wire that holds a spinner blade (Johnson Lures, Mankato, MN).

Bilge Pump - A pump that is usually situated at the lowest part of a boat to remove water from inside the hull.

Blue Crab (*Callinectes sapidus*) - Since it is an important food species, regulations govern the taking of blue crabs, which are also used by anglers as bait for catching cobia, drum, and tarpon.

* Blood Knot - A style of knot used to splice two lengths of fishing line or a line to a leader.

Bluefin Tuna (*Thunnus thynnus*) - The largest tuna, with short pectoral fins, a long, pointed head and relatively small eye. The fish is a very valuable commercial and game fish.

Bluefish (*Pomatamus saltatrix*) - A popular game fish, greenish or bluish above, silvery on the sides with a blackish blotch at the base of the pectoral fin. Bluefish have lots of very sharp teeth and powerful jaws.

Bonito, Atlantic (*Sarda sarda*) - A game fish that is bluish above and silvery below with dark stripe on the back. Also called striped bonito.

Bow light - The light on the front of a boat required by law to be visible at night. The left half of the light is red and the right half is green.

Bucktail Jig - A type of lure consisting of a lead-head jig tied with deer hair around the hook shank.

Bulkhead - An upright partition between compartments in a vessel or a wall built to retain earth along a shoreline.

Carolina Rig - Fishing terminal tackle consisting of an egg sinker threaded onto the main line above a swivel, a leader tied to the swivel and a hook tied to the leader.

Cast net - A circular net with lines radiating out from a center bearing called the "horn" to weights along the perimeter. After being cast onto a school of baitfish or shrimp, the weights are drawn together by a main line to hold the bait within the net.

Center console - A pedestal from which a boat is steered that can also contain instruments and storage areas and is located in the center of a boat.

Channel bass - Angler's name for red drum.

Chine - Small projections or ridges running front to back along the sides of the bottom of a boat to add rigidity and help guide the boat in a straight line. Chines may be used in place of a keel or in addition to a keel.

Chopper Blue - A large bluefish.

Cigar Minnow - Any of several species of cigar-shaped minnows that can be caught in ocean waters with multiple gold-hook feather jigs or cast nets and used as bait.

Clark Spoon - Trade name for a style of metal trolling lure (James E. Clark, Inc., St. Petersburg, FL).

Cleat - A metal or plastic T-shaped device attached to a deck or dock for the purpose of securing a boat with rope.

Click-type drag - A mechanical drag consisting of a metal spring and plastic or metal gears to create resistance to line being pulled from a reel by a hooked fish.

Clouser minnow - A style of fly with a weighted head that causes the hook to ride in a point up position.

Cobia (*Rachycentron canadum*) - An almost entirely brown game fish with a dark stripe running along the mid-side and blackish fins. Also called ling or lemonfish, cobia are strong fighters.

Copper-based anti-fouling paint - A type of paint that prevents plant and animal growth on a boat bottom primarily by having in its composition large amounts of copper, which is toxic to much marine life.

Cork friction pads - Pads made of natural cork from the bark of a cork oak used to create resistance in a drag mechanism to a line being pulled from a reel by a hooked fish.

Crappie (*Pomoxis nigromaculatus, annularis*) - Two species of small, freshwater game fish.

Croaker, Atlantic (*Micropogonias undulatus*) - A popular food fish having a silvery body with slightly diagonal, narrow dark lines or rows of spots above and spotted dorsal fins. The fish often makes an internal "croaking" sound when landed.

Deceiver - A style of neutral-weighted fishing fly that orients the hook point-down.

Depth recorder - An electrical device that uses the speed of a sound wave's echo to calculate a bottom depth and show it on a screen.

Downrigger - A device used to fish deep by attaching a fishing line to a release clip on a heavily weighted ball or planer that is connected to a cable wound onto a reel.

Drag - A mechanism on a fishing reel that controls the amount of pressure needed to release line while fighting a fish.

161

Drum, Black (*Pogonias cromis*) - A dark gray or brassy brown fish with 4-5 black bars that are widest on the back with the last bar stopping above the lateral line, and having many chin barbels. The dark bars may become indistinct in large adult fish. The fish often makes a loud, internal "drumming" sound when landed.

Drum, red (*Sciaenops ocellatus*) - Also called redfish, puppy drum, channel bass and spot-tail bass by anglers, the red drum is so popular it is North Carolina's state fish. Red drum are long and relatively slender, with bronze-colored bodies that are darker above than below, and typically have a distinct, black spot at the base of the tail. The fish often makes a loud, internal "drumming" sound when landed.

Eddy - A current that circles counter to the main current flow and may also be called a whirlpool.

Egg sinker - A fishing weight having an oval shape that is molded with a hole in the center through which line is threaded.

Encrustations - Marine growths usually caused by the shells of animals, especially oysters and barnacles.

False albacore (*Euthynnus alletteratus*) - A game fish that has diagonal, sometimes wavy, dark bars on each side of the back and 4-5 dark spots below the pectoral fin. Also called little tunny and spotted bonito.

Fast-scouring anti-fouling paint - A type of paint that prevents plant and animal growth on a boat bottom by gradually washing off when the boat is moving.

Fiddler Crab (*Uca sp.*) - Any of several species of small crabs in which the male has one enlarged claw. Fiddler crabs are numerous in grass beds and along estuary shorelines where they burrow into the mud. They make excellent bait for sheepshead and drum.

Fin-S - Trade name for a style of soft plastic tail generally used by hooking onto a jig (Lunker City Fishing Specialities, Meriden, CT).

Flatfish - Angler's term for flounder.

Float Rig - Fishing terminal tackle consisting of a float attached or sliding on a main line above a swivel, a leader tied to the swivel and a hook tied to the leader. Most saltwater float rigs are tied with one or more treble hooks.

Flounder (*Paralichthys sp.*) - A popular game and food fish having a flattened body and both eyes on the same side of the head. There are many species of flounder, with the southern, summer, and gulf flounder the most common species in the Carolinas.

Fore - Front area of a boat.

Fry - Small, juvenile fish.

Galvanic action - A chemical reaction creating electricity caused by direct contact between two different metals that can cause rapid corrosion of metal boat hulls and accessories.

Gibbs Minnow - Trade name for a heavy metal lure that is usually jigged up and down to attract fish (Gibbs Nortac, Burnsby, B.C., Canada).

Glass minnow - Angler's term for any of several species of minnow and fry that are tiny and transparent. Many very young fish are transparent.

Gold-hook rig - A rig having several small feather jigs with gold hooks used small to catch baitfish.

Got-cha - Trade name for a style of cylindrical metal lure that can be cast, jigged or trolled (Sea Striker, Morehead City, NC).

163

Graphite - A type of carbon added to the composition of a fishing rod to increase its sensitivity to the strike of a fish.

Gunwale - The upper edge of the side of a boat, also spelled gunnel.

Hatch cover - A door that covers a hole in the floor, side, or compartment of a boat.

Hopkins Spoon - Trade name for a type of metal fishing lure (Hopkins, Norfolk, VA).

Hull - The body of a boat, excluding appurtenances such as motors, masts and steering mechanisms.

Inline spinner - A spinner attached directly in front or behind and on the same axis as a lure body.

Islander - Trade name for a style of trolling lure consisting of plastic head and plastic skirt (Tournament Tackle, Inc., Satellite Beach, FL.)

Jetty - A structure of pilings, rocks, wood, steel or concrete that protects a harbor or inlet from waves or current erosion.

Keel - A projection running along the centerline of a boat to add rigidity and to help guide the boat in a straight line. Also the main support structure considered the backbone of a boat.

Killifish - See mud minnow.

Leadhead or Lead-head Jig - A lure of lead molded onto a hook that may or may not be tied with fur, feathers, artificial fibers or fitted with a plastic tail.

Live-bait rod - A relatively limber fishing rod designed to minimize its effect on the natural movement of a live baitfish.

Live well - A tank that keeps bait alive by the intake and discharge of water through the use of a pump.

Loran Coordinates - Location of a position established by triangulation of distances between any two of several shore-based navigational signal transmitters maintained by the U.S. government. Coordinates are determined by a receiver unit on a boat and are identified on widely available nautical charts. (Loran is being phased out in favor of a satellite-based transmitting system called Global Positioning System or GPS, used in the same manner as the Loran system.)

Menhaden, Atlantic (*Brevoortia tyrannus*) - A baitfish with brassy sides and a dark bluish green back and numerous spots on the side behind a dark shoulder spot that feeds by filtering plankton from seawater and congregates in large schools. Also called pogy, mossbunker, or fatback. Easy to catch in cast nets, menhaden are a preferred bait of saltwater anglers.

Mepps Comet - Trade name for a style of lure with an inline front spinning blade, a brass body, and a treble hook dressed with natural squirrel tail, plastic minnow imitation, or other material (Mepps, Antigo, WI).

MirrOlure - Trade name for a style of plastic minnow-imitating lure (L&S Bait Company, Largo, FL).

Mogambo Grub - Trade name for a style of large plastic grub tail usually hooked onto a jig (Kalin Company, Brawley, CA).

Monofilament line - A fishing line consisting of one strand of plastic.

Mud minnow - Also called killifish, mummichogs and gudgeons, three species are popular baitfish in the Carolinas. They can be caught in cast nets and traps. *Fundulus heteroclitus* is a greenish

165

minnow with yellow spangles, white spots and a white or yellow belly. *Fundulatus majalis* is a white minnow with distinct vertical or horizontal black lines. *Cyprinodon variegatus* is about one inch long with a neon blue nape and bright yellow- or pink-edged fins.

* **Nail Knot** - A style of knot used to connect a leader to a fly line.

Neoprene glove - A glove made of foam rubber widely used by fishermen in cold weather.

Pigfish (*Orthopristis chrysoptera*) - A gray colored fish, often with a bluish cast and bronze to yellowish spots, dashes and other small markings. Pigfish are common bait stealers and are not considered to be good eating by most anglers. They make good bait for a variety of game fish. The fish makes an internal sound like the "oink" of a pig when landed, giving its angler's name.

Pinfish (*Lagodon rhomboides*) - A fish with a dark shoulder spot centered on the lateral line and four dark, obscure crossbars on the sides. Considered a nuisance by many anglers, pinfish are easy to catch and make good bait for a variety of fish. Spines along the fins are erected for defense and easily puncture human skin, earning the fish its name.

Planer - A metal or plastic device that uses the pressure of moving water to carry a lure or bait to a greater depth than if it were fished alone.

Plastic grub tail - An artificial lure made of plastic designed to imitate a baitfish or shrimp when fitted onto a lead-head jig.

Plugging rod - A fishing rod designed for casting artificial lures.

Ply the brine - Author's poetic expression for fishing in saltwater.

Pompano, Florida (*Trachinotus carolinus*) - A deep-bodied, silvery fish with a dark back and yellowish belly, anal and tail fins that is prized for its gourmet qualities.

Pork rind - A style of natural bait made from the skin of a pig that is attached to a jig or spoon to provide an enticing action for catching game fish.

Rapala **stick minnow** - Trade name for a style of wooden lure that is long and narrow and imitates an injured minnow (Normark, Galloway, Ireland).

Rat-L-Trap - Trade name for a style of crankbait (Bill Lewis Lures, Alexandra, LA).

Rebel **stick minnow** - Trade name for a style of plastic lure that is long and narrow and imitates an injured minnow (Rebel Fort Smith, AR).

Redfish - Angler's name for red drum.

Resin-bodied fly with artificial dressings - Style of fly having a plastic body molded onto a hook with plastic fibers tied to the body or hook shank.

Revolving spool reel - A fishing reel that holds line on a spool that revolves perpendicular to the rod. Also called bait-casting reel since it was originally used specifically for casting bait in the days before artificial lures were developed for casting.

Riprap seawall - A wall constructed of stones to protect an area from erosion caused by wave action or currents.

Rock Crab (*Panopeus herbstii*) - A small crab found in the mud of oyster beds and beneath rocks. Also called mud crabs, they make excellent bait for sheepshead and drum.

Rooster Tail - Trade name for a style of lure with an inline front spinning blade, metal body and treble hook dressed with feathers (Yakima Bait Co., Granger, WA).

Rope - Many types of rope are used to secure boats at moorings or while at anchor. The most popular modern rope materials are Nylon or polypropylene.

Sandbar - A submerged or emerged dune or ridge of sand created by waves or currents.

Scupper Valve - A gutter in a boat hull used to channel water is called a scupper. A one-way flap or ball valve situated at the end of a scupper to let water drain and closing to prevent water from coming into the boat is called a scupper valve.

Sea-run striper - A wild striped bass that makes a spawning run from the ocean to inland waters as opposed to a striped bass artificially raised and stocked in a landlocked lake.

Sea Witch - Trade name for a style of synthetic skirt that is used as a dressing to a natural trolling bait (C&H Lures, Jacksonville, FL).

Self-bailing deck - A style of boat deck having drain holes to let water run off above the waterline.

Setting the hook - Moving a fishing rod to drive the point of a hook into a fish.

Shrimp - Small marine crustacean that swims or crawls by using paired legs or swims by using a fan-like tail that propels it rapidly backward. Some species are used as human food and bait for catching fish.

Shrimp Ball - A mixture of clay and pet food placed in salt water to attract shrimp for catching with a cast net.

Silversides, Atlantic (*Menidia menidia* and other *Menidia sp.*) - A small, schooling fish of coastal waters, greenish above, pale below, usually with a prominent silver strip along the side.

Sit-down Console - A pedestal from which a boat is steered that can also contain instruments and storage areas and can be seen over while sitting on a chair-sized seat.

Skinny water - Author's term for shallow water.

Skunk - An angler's term meaning he hasn't caught any fish.

Slip sinker - A fishing weight through which fishing line slides.

Snapper Blue - A small bluefish.

Spanish mackerel (*Scromberomorus maculatus*) - A slender game fish with many large, dark brown and brassy spots. The lateral line slopes evenly downward with no sudden drop below the second dorsal fin.

Speckled trout (*Cynoscion nebulosus*) - Anglers' name for spotted sea trout, a popular game fish that is bluish gray above, silvery to whitish below with many black spots on the upper side, second dorsal fin and tail fin.

Spider-web lines - Ultra-light monofilament fishing line, generally anything less than six-pound breaking strength or a line that is extremely undersized for its intended catch.

Spinning reel - A fishing reel with a fixed spool oriented parallel to the rod that has a bail revolving around the reel to retrieve line. Also called an open-faced reel.

Stingsilver - Trade name for a heavy metal lure that is usually jigged up and down to attract fish (Haw River Tackle, Burlington, NC).

Striped bass (*Morone saxatilis*) - A silvery game fish having seven to eight black stripes along the sides. Also called linesider.

Structure - A fisherman's term meaning any manmade or natural object that projects from the bottom or shoreline which attracts fish.

Surface popper - A style of floating or semi-floating fishing lure with a flat or concave head. Retrieved in short jerks, it makes a popping sound that attracts fish.

* Surgeon's loop - A style of knot at the end of a fly line used to connect a fly to a leader or a leader to a fly line.

Swirl - A curl or twist counter to the main current.

Swivel - A metal device with a bearing used to prevent line twist and to connect a line to a leader or lure.

Tarpon (*Megalops atlanticus*) - A silver game fish with a dark green or bluish back with bony scales.

Three-rod method - Author's technique for using three rods to present lures and baits at different depths and to quickly find biting game fish.

3/0 weedless Kahle hook - This example sequence describes a certain hook; 3/0 refers to hook size, weedless shows it is equipped with a spring weed-guard, Kahle refers to the type, which in this example is a wide-bend hook used for holding live baits and projecting the hook point deeply into the mouth of the game fish. All hooks are numbered and described on their packaging.

Tinsel jig - A type of jig with a shiny or clear plastic skirt.

Tippet - Terminal portion of a fly-fishing leader.

Transom - Top of the rear wall of a boat.

Treble hook - A style of fishing hook with three points projecting from a single shank.

Trolling - A method of fishing in which the lure or bait is dragged through the water by a moving boat.

Yo-zuri - Trade name for a plastic, minnow-imitating lure (Tachibana, Takeo, Japan).

*Most fishing line manufacturers furnish knot tying instructions with their spools of line. There are also books that illustrate the tying of fishing knots readily available at most tackle shops.

About the Author

Mike Marsh is one of the most prolific and popular outdoor writers in North Carolina. An award-winning writer since his first book, *Carolina Hunting Adventures – Quest for the Limit*, was published in 1995, he has written hundreds of articles and columns about hunting and fishing. He is a member of the Outdoor Writer's Association of America and a member the Southeastern Outdoor Press Association.

At the time *Inshore Angler* was first published, he had served the sporting community as an outdoor columnist for the Wilmington *Star News* and Tabor City-Loris *Tribune* for five years and as Southeast Regional Editor of *Carolina Adventure* magazine for five years. He contributes outdoor-related articles and news columns to *Carolina Adventure, North Carolina Game and Fish, North Carolina Sportsman, Carolina Sportsman's Journal, Wildlife in North Carolina* and other regional and national magazines.

Always an avid outdoorsman, he hunted and fished during his childhood and teenage years in Guilford County, North Carolina. After earning an associate degree in Fish and Wildlife Management from Wayne Community College in Goldsboro, he was employed by the North Carolina Division of Environmental Management in Mooresville.

After living a hunting and fishing life on Lake Norman for five years, he moved to Wilmington in 1978 along with his wife, Carol. Their son, Justin, was born in 1983. The family's hunting and fishing adventures have been the sources for many of the articles written by both Mike and Carol.